By Choice

I CHOSE TO BE A... COP.

K. HENSLEY

Support the Thin Blue Line

Kerry Hensley

2017

Chapter 1

Let me begin by giving a little background into my life prior to law enforcement. I was part of a family-owned business headed up by my father. He started this business after a short partnership with an individual he called a friend. However a friend he wasn't, as he made decisions without consulting my father concerning the operations and financial situations of the business. This all occurred after my father built a reputation as one of top masonry job foreman around the Houston area.

Seems he was sent to every job the large company bid that was possibly underbid. If anyone could pull a profit out of an underbid job, it was my father. Of course, being that good and dedicated also meant that our family had to travel. Though most of his work was in Houston, he was sent to many other areas as well as other states to bring these jobs in under budget.

Growing up I was able to live in several states, each time returning to Houston after a job was completed. We even lived in Cocoa Beach, Florida during the early 60's while he was building Cape Canaveral. We were there when President Kennedy was assassinated.

I attended different schools throughout elementary and junior high, but we all adapted well and seemed to make friends anywhere we lived. My youngest brother was born in Louisiana while my father was on one of these... shall I call them adventures? My second brother and I were born in Texas. As a matter of fact, my father was building a new wing on a downtown Houston hospital while my brother was being born inside that same hospital. Certainly, that doesn't happen very often. One of the downfalls of moving around is changing houses so often. I don't ever remember living in a bad house; as a matter of fact, all the homes were nice and comfortable for our family. Each time we returned to Houston, we lived in a different home. We were always afforded with, as I called them, "really neat things."

At one house my father... let me stop with the father business. He was my dad and Dad is what we called him. Anyway, at this one house in South Houston, we had the very first color television in the neighborhood. I remember when my dad brought it home in his pickup from Sears and as he pulled up, the neighbors began to gather around to get a look at this thing. He got it all set up in our living room and turned it on. WOW... it was like having the movies right at home, in color! Everyone was amazed at the beautiful picture. So now, all we needed were more shows filmed in color to watch because most weekly shows were still in black and white. Then it hit us; there was a show going to start soon and it was in color. Everyone went to their own homes, got whatever they needed and returned to find a place to sit. All the kids were excited, and to tell the truth, so were the grownups, to get to see this new show and it was in color to boot.

Then the show started... Na Na Na Na Na Na Na Na Na "Pow!" "Zap" "Crrrrrunch" Batman... Batman... "Blam" Batman... Batman "punch". That's right, *Batman* starring Adam West and man did it look real! This may have been the coolest day ever in my life. Of course after that, more and more neighbors started buying color sets and our reign as the only family with the color television leveled off.

As a family, we loved watching all the "old classics" from *Andy Griffith Show* to *Gunsmoke*. What may have been my first desire to become a police officer began with the 1960's cop shows. The pattern here was that nearly everything I watched and really liked seemed to be police themed shows, either a dramatic series or a comedy show… it didn't matter to me. The one thing Hollywood never ran out of was cop shows. They were on all the time most every night and I liked them.

I sometimes wonder what it was that I actually liked about those TV cops. Was it because they carried guns? Was it because they had cool cars or drove fast? Was it because they seemed to make things better, and of course in the 60's, they always won? You never saw Matt Dillon lose. Even though it might have seemed that all hope was lost, Matt found a way to win by the time the show ended.

All the 60's cops were good. Think about it if you are old enough… even *Car 54* found a way to best the bad guys. I liked this stuff. I thought these guys were the coolest people in the world and I wanted to be like them.

With the Vietnam War on the news every night, I began watching reports of protest. At that time of my life, I didn't really understand the war or the effects it had on our country. I saw police holding back angry people and sometimes even hitting them with sticks or spraying them with high pressure hoses. What was going on here? Why was all this happening? This was not like any of the shows I watched and I began thinking that maybe the cops weren't the good guys after all. Now I was really confused, but at that age I woke up in a different world every morning and that sort of thing wasn't happening close to me... so for Halloween in 1968, I dressed as a Hippie (look it up if you don't know what that is) protesting the police.

The following year we moved to Bethany, Oklahoma for another one my dad's jobs.

The 60's opened up a whole new world to me, I was in the eighth grade and of course pretty much knew everything except I really didn't know anything. I begin moving away from the cop shows I once loved and started watching shows like *Then Came Bronson* and dreamt of riding motorcycles all over the country. I saw *Easy Rider* and Peter Fonda became a hero. I also started to dislike the police. I am not sure now as to why I did, just because everyone else did. They hated the Government including the president and anyone that had any authority over them. They hated the War and believe or not... the soldiers who fought it! Names were tagged to the soldiers as "Baby Killers" and the Government became "The Man." They even had a name for the police and so now they were the "Pigs."

Still in the eighth grade and in Oklahoma I started to think about a career but only because it was required in school. Part of a class assignment was to think of what we wanted to do and develop a plan to get to that position. Not one person in my class chose Peace Officer... especially me. I was going to become a Dentist, why? I don't know. All I remember was that my dad told me that a dentist made lots of money and didn't have to deal with weather like he did; so... Dentist it was. Looking back, I never really cared about dentistry but it made my dad happy and I cared about his opinions.

One day my dad brought home a small Honda motorcycle... wow... I could be like Bronson on my Honda 50. He taught my brother and me how to ride this machine by going around and around and around the parking lot of the apartment we lived in. He taught us well and safety was his number one concern. We practiced for hours and hours, day after day with him on the back guiding us the whole way. Then… he brought home another Honda, a 65 and it was mine because I was the oldest. I remember thinking "I am so cool, I ride a motorcycle, I am going to make lots of money … I am going to be like Dr. Steve Kiley on *Marcus Welby M.D.* (Again, look it up if you don't remember) So as you can tell, the pattern forming here is that I was influenced so far by my dad and selected television shows. Good or bad that's the way it was.

Oh yeah, let's not forget the girls because they were now a major part in the ways that my brain was traveling. Where were these girls a few years ago? I didn't notice them like this but now, damn! Those Saturdays at the roller rink, holding hands and listening to *Venus* and *Spirit in the Sky.* Let's not leave out Credence Clearwater Revival, Tommy James and the Shondells and of course, Jagger and the boys. Then something happened to me… Hendrix, Cream and this guy named Eric Clapton, as well as the new style music that The Beatles were putting out. I loved this stuff, could hardly stand not to be listening to it. I even got a guitar so I could learn to be like these guys.

What happened to the motorcycle riding dentist? Well, he must have ridden into the sunset because a motorcycle riding Rock Star was way cooler and had a lot more girls involved. It's a shame I never truly learned to play that guitar very well because I would have liked to have given the lifestyle a try… me and ten million other people!

Enter the 70's and back to Houston when we moved into yet another house as well as another school. I was going to start high school; hell; I was grown and definitely knew everything about everything. I was now old enough to have a motorcycle license and my dad bought me a Honda 90… I could ride it to school (illegally of course) because at the time I was only legal to have a five-brake horsepower or 5BHP motorcycle. All I had to do was not get caught by them "dumb ass" police and everything would be fine. Even though I was unable to park on school property, this became a way of life every morning and afternoon. I didn't have a proper license so I could not get a parking permit and therefore we, yes, we (there were many of us in the same predicament) parked across a street in an empty lot.

The day did finally arrive that I got a license and a bigger motor-cycle as well…a 350 Honda. At that time I thought it was one bad machine and I loved the bike. Still illegal, so I had to continue to park it across the street, until one day I came out of school and it was gone. That's right… stolen, the only bike of the bunch that was miss-ing. With 30-40 to choose from, why did some asshole take mine? Time to call the police, they will find it… in Houston… right?

Needless to say, the police never found my motorcycle and I cursed them with some pretty good multi-syllable words because they were supposed to be able to do these simple things. I really talked bad about them and the truth was, most likely they never looked. One motorcycle, five million people… bye-bye motorcycle.

Still not old enough to drive a car, once again my dad worked out a way for me to obtain another bike… work for it. Hmmm, never tried that before so let's give it a try. He had me start going to a once-a-week night trade school to learn how to become a brick-layer. I worked during the summertime for his company at mini-mum wage as well as some weekends with him. I finally, with his help, got another motorcycle and was back on the road. This new bike was a wheelie machine and I tried to ride on the back tire as often as possible.

A friend of mine bought the same size, style and color motorcycle as I had and several teens in the area matched them as well. One day on my way to another friend's house to meet up with several others, I came around a corner and pulled the front end up and started my wheelie. When I set the front tire down. I saw the Houston Police car turn the corner and turn on his lights. Crap… what am I going to do now? If I get a ticket from this "Pig", my dad will take away my bike so I turned the throttle and got to my friend's house way before the officer showed up. I parked the bike next to its twin, and because he had just arrived, his engine was still hot too.

We had gone into the garage and replaced our helmets with some others and had just sat down when the HPD cruiser turned the corner. He pulled up to where we were and wanted to know who just ran from him, to which we replied "What?" We told him we had been there only a short time but had come in from the opposite direction. When he said he was looking for a bike that color but the rider was wearing a red, white and blue helmet, my friend told him that someone on a bike like ours with that color helmet had just came through there in a hurry. He looked at us sort of funny and squinting his eyes before driving off. We thought, "What a stupid cop" and laughed about that the rest of the day. Looking back now, I think he knew but he gave us a break. Still, we laughed at him then. This happened about the time pictures from Kent State started appearing and hatred for the police and the military was dangerously high.

Chapter 2

Sixteen could not come fast enough and I, again with the help of my dad, got a car. A good looking 1966 red Mustang with wide tires and chrome rims. It had a Hypo 289 with 4-speed transmission and best of all… an 8-track tape deck. (Again, look it up if you don't know). The war in Vietnam was over, tensions were settling down, and I was off the motorcycles and roaming the streets with Derek and the Dominoes and The Allman Brothers blasting as loud as possible for them days. Along with the car, a few other things started appearing in my life and a few of them were illegal. Yes, I said it… alcohol and the evil weed known as marijuana. Now first of all, I was never a big user of either; however, I always seemed to wind up with those who were. I was always afraid of the cops, but of course I always acted like I wasn't, you know… "I ain't skeered."

One afternoon when school let out, a good friend had an accident on one of the streets next to the parking lot. I saw his vehicle and stopped to see if he was alright. As I approached him, he grabbed a pouch (looked like a bank bag today) and handed it to me. He told me to hang on to it and he would get it later. Can anyone see the STUPID here? I placed it in my front seat and shortly after the cops arrived. Damn police… they gave him a ticket just because he pulled out in front of someone. These cops sure do pick on teenagers and we are tired of it!

My buddy, my friend, continued trying to tell me to get away from there and finally it dawned on me… What's in that pouch? I walked over and looked inside… Holy Shit, there was dope in that pouch and it was in my car while two police officers are right here. These assholes are going to arrest me because they like to arrest teenagers and ruin their lives. How could anyone be a cop? What sort of mentally ill, insane person wants to be like that? I got in my car and slowly rolled away thinking, "Wow that was close." Now, for a place to hide this stuff until my friend was finished up with them cops. How about under the seat? Yes, that's the perfect place to hide things. Do you still see the STUPID going on here?

That little episode did work out for me and I took the credit for outsmarting the police, but I never took another pouch or bag or box from anyone again. Truth is… that scared the crap out of me. Well, this situation did happen again, only the weed was in someone's pocket while they were in my car… okay. The truth… more than just one time. I want to give alcohol its time as well, but it was almost always beer because we never had enough money to get the hard stuff.

There was the guy we all knew and he was 21 so… hello beer. For a six pack, he would buy us all we had the money for and this was every weekend. We had woodsies (party on someone's property we didn't know) or we drove to Galveston and partied on the beach. Not the cleaned up beach you might find today but the old dirty Galveston beach… nasty! To sum it up, we always found a place to go and because we were so much smarter than the cops, we never got caught. All of our parents didn't have a clue… oh; they weren't as smart as the cops.

We did have a woodsie one night and talked our girlfriends into concocting a slumber party lie so they could be there too. We received word that one girl's father was on his way and he was mad, plus he had the law with him. We panicked and took the girls to another area before he arrived. Wow… when he arrived was he ever mad. Not only was he mad, but he had brought all the fathers with him… they were all upset.

This may have been the first time in my teenage years that I witnessed a cop doing something nice for me. This one officer took control of that situation and not only calmed the parents down, he got us to tell the truth and go and get the girls. He stood there and told the angry fathers that they should take a moment and remember back when they were our age and the things they did. He reminded them that nobody was hurt and nothing had happened and everyone went home without any more problems.

Now what did all this mean? Did real cops actually do nice things? Do real cops really care about people and what happens to them? All this got me to thinking that maybe they weren't so bad after all. That would all get tested during my senior year that started in the fall of 1973. By this time I had a constant girlfriend so getting into difficult situations came less and less. I had gotten a new car, but only because my parents had moved to Nacogdoches (again for some more of Dad's jobs at SFASU) and allowed me to stay in Houston so I could graduate with my classmates of four years. There were plenty of restrictions and lots of strings attached, but the decision was made. My grandparents were building a retirement home up in Rusk and traveled there every weekend, so I had the weekends to myself as well as the occasional week days they were gone.

I was given the new car, a Plymouth Duster, so I would be able to make the trip to Nacogdoches at least once a month to see my mom. Dad didn't want to say it, but the visits were for them and me because I did miss them. My parents were great and always went way beyond what most would do for their three boys. They were understanding and yet firm with rules. A perfect example is when I first received my driver's license I was 16 and lived in one of largest cities in the country… of course, I had a curfew. My car was to be parked in the driveway by 10 PM every night including weekends. Now I thought this was the worst and most cruel rule ever, but looking back, it may be why I'm around today. My parents told me as I became a better driver, they would increase the time allowed on the streets. Remember how smart I was? Smarter than the police and certainly wiser than my parents…you know, they were old and didn't know how the world worked.

Anyway… I was out one Friday night and was having fun with a friend and our girlfriends and noticed it was getting close to 10 o'clock. I started taking everyone home (They had to be home at 10:00 as well) and when I was ready to head home… oops it was 10:00. Son of a bitch, what will I do now? I know… lie. Remember we didn't have cell phones back then, so I came up with a story that would work because I just made it up and nobody knew it but me. Are you ready for this? Really? Okay, I set my watch back 10 minutes. I got this! I'm good to go. Dad will never figure this out… "Damn, I'm smart."

I pulled in the driveway and noticed my dad standing on the porch with his arms crossed. This was not a good sign but my plan was perfect so no worries. I sort of jumped out of my car and looked at my watch… "Whew, just made it, that was close." He never broke an expression; he just held out his hand and said, "Keys." Now was the perfect time for my plan and I told him it was just now 10:00 and turned my watch towards him for him to see that I made it. He placed the keys in his pocket, grinned and very calmly said, "That didn't work for me either." Then he walked in the house. It took a week to get them back… who'd a thunk it? Maybe the old man wasn't so dumb after all.

So back to what I was explaining before… my first trip from Houston to Nacogdoches was a strange adventure. Not so much the drive up, it was just a drive, but as I arrived in Nacogdoches, I got turned around and while I was searching for some apartments on North Street, I wound up on a construction road that would soon be University Drive. I have no clue how I got on that dusty, uncompleted road but I needed to find a way off of it. There were barricades everywhere, blinking lights, large piles of gravel and all sorts of tractors and road equipment… everywhere. Did I mention there were several signs advising me not to be there as well? But again, I could not find a way off of the area. Finally there seemed to be a way out close to the university and I drove until I was on pavement again. I still had no idea of where I was and certainly didn't know where I was going.

I had only seen the apartment complex one time… heck I didn't even know the name of them, only what they looked like. I was sitting still and trying to get my bearings straight and who pulls up behind me…? The Nacogdoches Police with lights flashing. This is a good thing; he can direct me to the apartments because I am definitely lost. As I sat there waiting for this officer to walk up to my window, I wasn't thinking about anything except how to get to Mom and Dad's so I could eat and rest from the drive.

I had Trapeze playing Medusa on the old 8-Track and it may have been a little too loud. I had let my hair grow out a little and maybe it was a little too long. So... as this officer approached my window he asked me for my driver's license and I leaned over to get my billfold from my right rear pocket. All I heard was, "No, No, No, don't do anything stupid!" I still had not seen his face and did not know what I was doing was stupid. I started to turn my head towards him and felt something against my cheek... it was the barrel of his revolver. I damn near shit on myself! I had never been that scared before and just froze up... luckily, I didn't start calling for my mommy.

Now I was from Houston where a lot of crime occurs, even back then, and had been pulled over many times by the Houston Police but never had a gun pulled on me before. This officer told me to remove my billfold slowly and hand him my license. I did so and when I moved my head again he had removed his gun. He asked me what I was doing in his town and what was I transporting up from Houston. When he decided I wasn't transporting drugs and was really lost, he directed me to the apartments. Oh, how I hated that cop... all cops! "Your town, my ass, I will kick your ass... how do you like that?" I said after he drove off.

After a great visit with the folks I headed back to Houston, my girlfriend and good ol' J. Frank Dobie High School. Get back to my part time job at J C Penney (more than just a clothing store then) and away from Nacogdoches and the crazy effin' (cleaned that up for readers) cops that worked there. Not more than three weeks later after leaving the Village Inn Pizza on Market Square, I was pulled over again.

Village Inn was a pizza parlor that brought in live bands and served beer to just about anyone wanting some. I was never asked for an ID during the entire time I was going there. Lots and lots of Dobie students showed up at Village Inn even though it was in Downtown and several miles from our neighborhoods. I had three friends in my car and one of them wanted to stop and buy some beer for later and he knew a place he could get it. Do you feel that "Stupid" coming on again? I stopped; he bought three six packs and we were on our way to our side of town. No problem… right? As I exited I45 onto Fuqua, you will never guess who was there? A Houston police officer and he did pull me over.

I don't know why he stopped me, and back then you didn't ask. He approached the car, seemed fine and wanted to know where we had been and where we were going. He shined his flashlight in the back and asked, "What is this?" Well, crap again… not even my beer, but it was in my car. He had us, we were busted and we figured he was about to take us in, but instead he started laughing and asked what should we do about this. You know how you always got that one friend that just has to talk at the wrong moment? That friend was in my car and he told the officer that he could just let us go and keep the beer. But you know, that cop had a better idea… he had us open every single can and pour them out… in the back floorboard of my new car. It was that or go to jail, but at least we got to make the choice. After all, how bad could it be? We could just go clean it up and be done… wrong!

Getting the beer out was no problem; getting the smell out a few days later was awful. It took over a month to completely get the beer odor out of that car. Oh, my goodness, did I ever hate cops now with a passion. I'm sure I threatened to kick that cop's ass too… but the threat would also have been said after he drove off.

The rest of High School went fairly easily for me as I had good grades, good teachers and lots of friends that I still run across today. One of those teachers was absolutely, hands down the finest teacher I ever knew (I still keep in touch with her today). Football games, cheerleaders and Friday night parties were the new interests in my life and I was having the best year of my life. However, there was that incident when a group of us decided to ride our motorcycles to Galveston.

Although most of the group were driving cars, very few trucks back then, those motorcycles were still around and we did take an occasional short trip on them. We surely must have been a sight, a bunch of teenagers wearing Hobie shirts, Levis and desert boots (remember?) riding Japanese-made motorcycles... trying to be cool like the bikers of that era. I am quite sure that somewhere, someone did mistake us for "Easy Rider." That day there were around twenty, maybe twenty-five bikes all running south towards Galveston. We were not moving too fast because some of those bikes had no more than 125cc engines. We tried to stay on the service roads as long as possible but had to enter I45 at times. The bikes ranged from a 125 up to a 750 and nobody cared because we were having fun.

I was aboard my trusty Kawasaki 500 H1 and it was fast, really fast with lots of quick power. Several of the guys started pulling wheelies on the freeway. I45 was not that big in the 70's and this particular day there wasn't a lot of traffic, so why not? This could be fun, so up with my front end as well. That wheelie must have been one of my best ever and couldn't have happened at a better time... right in front of all my riding buddies... wrong!

I was just going along and heard a familiar sound... whoop, whoop, whoop. I set the front end down and what did I see? You guessed it, flashing lights of the Texas Highway Patrol... Crap again! The way my luck had run with the law, I knew I was getting a ticket for sure. I pulled over to the side of the freeway as all the guys kept going but only about a hundred yards when they all pulled over. That was really cool to see and I remember smiling before I turned to see the biggest person I think I had ever seen. Think of him as a JJ Watt on steroids in a DPS uniform. He had a ticket book in hand and I told myself, "Be cool and don't do anything stupid, take the ticket and go."

He got up beside me and asked me to please step off my motorcycle and remove my helmet. He asked for my driver's license and I obliged him. I was prepared for the speech, I was prepared for a scolding, I was prepared for the ticket that I would have to explain to my dad... the only thing I wasn't prepared for is what he said and did.

This big burly Trooper with a chew of tobacco in his jaw turned his head and spit, then turned back to me and said, "You kept that one up a long time Mr. Lone Ranger." What? I really didn't know what he meant, so I said, "Excuse me, sir, I don't understand." His reply was priceless and I remember it word for word even today. It went like this. "Young man, I have been watching you and your buddies up there for a few miles. I saw all the raring up of them front tires like the Lone Ranger does with Silver. You just happened to be the one I stopped. Do you know how dangerous that is and what could happen to you if you fell off at that speed? What I should do is write a ticket, I should write you all tickets but I'm not going to do that. I'm going to tell you one thing and let you go on your way. Your momma doesn't deserve to have someone like me come to her home and tell her she has lost her kid in an accident and I've had to do that this week already".

I looked at this man and he was tearing up but never broke down. "Now git… and no more foolishness on these roads." I didn't know what to say to that… "Yes sir, and I will let them know," is all that came out. I rode up to the rest of the guys and they were laughing and joking about me being stopped, but it didn't take long for them to realize I wasn't laughing and that something was wrong. One friend asked if I was ok and I told him no… that officer had to tell some mom her kid had died. I told them I was going home because I didn't feel like going to Galveston anymore. I got turned north and headed home while the rest of them continued on south. That was my last motorcycle trip to Galveston as a teenager and I would not do it again until I was somewhere around 40, when I went through my "gotta have a Harley 'cause everybody-has-a-Harley stage."

I can't tell you how long I thought about that stop… but it hit me hard and I didn't even know the kid who died, I didn't know this momma, so why did I care so much? And just who was this officer that put this in my head? He acted like he cared but he was a cop and they don't care about anything but ruining someone's day. Things sure were changing… well, it's about time. There is no way that I was changing. I didn't have any use for police officers and that was that! But I was changing, and the next few years would prove to be a turning point in the way I thought and the way I acted.

Chapter 3

I look back these days at those high school years and have the best of memories. I had a diploma, I graduated with a 3.9 GPA, I had a nice car as well as a nice motorcycle and I was eligible to go to several colleges. I had good friends, many who would be for a lifetime; I had everything going for me, nothing in my way to the future except… Me! I had no clue what I wanted to do or for that matter, what direction I even thought of going. Seems all the professions I liked when I was younger, I was no longer interested in. I didn't want to go to school for at least a little while because I wanted a break. The only thing that I felt was certain was I had a girlfriend, and I guess that's all that mattered then.

Needless to say, that girlfriend wouldn't last and after trying many odd jobs as well as living in my own apartment, I surrendered and called my parents. I had sold my nice car to raise money but had bought an older vehicle that was mechanically sound and sort of a hot rod. I felt like the world had defeated me at 19 and running home to Mom and Dad with my tail tucked between my legs may not have been noble, but I sure was happy when they told me to come home.

Let me explain a few of my odd jobs before I move on because you may find yourself reliving your own first real jobs. Now remember, I knew how to be a bricklayer but everything in Houston was multi-story and I was afraid of heights. And besides all that, even though I truly admired my dad, I didn't want to do what he did for a living, so I went to work for a company that built cooling systems for off-shore rigs and it was right on the ship channel. I was going to get rich... $4.00 an hour... I would be buying a house in River Oaks soon. If you are not familiar with River Oaks, Google it and look at Mansions. I went to work every morning in the dark and came home every evening after dark. There was no time to do anything else.

It took several months for me to figure out that this was not what I thought it was. There was barely money left after all the bills to even go to McDonalds and eat. I stayed exhausted all the time and very seldom went to visit my parents. I sold my motorcycle to raise money, then my dirt bike; I was going downhill financially, so I went to work for Home Depot, then I tried K-mart, then Target. It seemed nothing I tried was going to get me in that River Oaks house any time in my near future. I finally found a job at Robertson Tank Lines on Monument Road for $5.25 per hour.

I saw the Battleship Texas and San Jacinto Monument every day for quite a few months. Both sort of lost their luster after a while. The great thing was, I wasn't working every minute of daylight and the route I took to and from work was pretty much cop free. I may have driven a little fast... I don't remember. After a few weeks of driving back and forth I stopped in at this little Mom & Pop type place for breakfast and as I entered I saw what? You got it... two police officers having their breakfast. I didn't see any squad cars outside... do police officers have other cars? Of course they do and these two guys were about to head in for the workday.

As I walked past trying not to make any type of eye contact one of the officers spoke, "Good morning, how are you today?" I was shocked but did reply to him, and then he said, "What type of mufflers are you using?" He told me he had some sort of glass packs on his and it sounded good too. He said they heard me every morning driving by and were glad to finally meet me. Really? Am I in trouble I asked myself, do I get a ticket now? What? The officer invited me to sit with them and have breakfast and guess what...? I did.

Over the next few months I had breakfast with those officers many times. I would do most of the listening while they talked about the events they had each day. I would ask questions and they would answer them until a friendship developed between two cops and... Me. I learned that these were just everyday guys with families very similar to my own. They gathered at Christmas time the same way we did. They had siblings just like mine and most of all... they were humans with feelings and emotions. I became fascinated with their stories and often thought how cool of a job that would be. These guys weren't the animals I had once thought but rather the opposite; they cared for the wellbeing of so many others even though sometimes they had to arrest someone. They didn't write tickets to ruin a teenager's life; they did it to save that life. They told me of some of the bad things they had experienced as well... vehicle accidents involving fatalities, shootings, rapes and not to forget, the drug dealers. I was able to actually look at things much differently after some of those mornings; was I getting smarter? No... I was growing up.

This stop became so much a part of my daily routine I was shocked one Monday morning when I arrived and they weren't there. I went ahead and ordered my meal expecting them to walk in any second. When I finished, they had still not arrived so I shrugged it off and went on to work. At work I started hearing about a shooting that had taken place the day before and that a police officer had been shot along with a civilian. It took place at an apartment complex in the afternoon and there was no word on the condition of the officer or resident and I remember thinking… No way, just no way. I stopped and bought a newspaper on the way home and read it cover to cover without finding any information about a shooting. Remember there were no cell phones and no internet so basically… nothing. I spent that evening wondering about my new friends and convincing myself that neither of them could be involved.

The next morning I stopped for breakfast and mentioned to the waitress about the situation. She seemed pretty upset and then told me it was one of them involved. Oh, Hell No!!!!! How was he? She had no recent news and said he had gone into surgery. Why? Why? Why would anybody shoot this officer? He is one of the coolest people around. He has a Dodge Charger with loud pipes, he rides motorcycles and… well, why?

I was worried for the rest of the week with no news coming my way and I stopped every morning to see if anything was coming in but nothing new was said. I still could not understand why anyone would do this. They must not have known he was great person, must not have known he loved his mom… wait, that was it, he had told me the name of the street his mom lived on and it was only a few miles away. The following day I called in sick…cough cough, hack hack…and went searching for this house. It took me a little while but I finally saw a house and there was his Dodge Charger in the driveway. I pulled up along the curb and parked but I could not force myself out of the car. What if he had died? What would I say? I had never been in any situation like this before and to be honest, I remember being scared.

I just sat there in my car like a zombie, only I had ZZ Top playing on the 8-track. It seemed like hours to me but truth was, it was only about twenty minutes or so before a lady walked outside and down to my car. Dang… this could have been my own mother, although maybe a few years older. She introduced herself to me and told me that my friend had been watching me from the window and wanted me to come inside. OK… he was alive and I felt a moment of relief but was reluctant to go in. She finally got me in and I heard, "Heard those pipes way down the street, thought it might be you. Come on in here." When I walked in that room and saw him smiling even though he had his arm in a sling and all bandaged up, I settled down and listened to his story of what had happened.

He first off told me our other friend was not involved in any way. These officers were not partners, just good friends that worked for the same department on the same shift. He said he responded with other officers to a domestic disturbance call in an apartment complex. He told me that when they arrived, voices could be heard and a lot of yelling and cursing. He was first in line and announced to the apartment that the police had arrived and to please step outside. He said a female yelled to help her and a male voice responded that the first person through the door would get shot. They talked back and forth for a while and finally my friend heard a gunshot and felt a burning pain in his elbow. The man had shot through the door and the bullet hit a brick wall and ricocheted into his elbow. He told me that the other officers got in the apartment and during the scuffle the "bad guy" was shot.

Both of them should make full recoveries. That was the last time I saw him because I left to move home with my family before he went back to work. I have often thought of the two officers and I am so glad that I was able to meet them. Realizing that cops are just normal people with an unusual job that could be dangerous, even deadly, but rewarding at the same time. Maybe being a cop wasn't that bad. If I was one, I would definitely want to be like them. I look back now and know that I admired those guys a lot and I also know they had a huge impact on my future decision to attend a police academy.

I didn't include any names in this story, not because I don't want you knowing… it's purely out of respect for those involved. I don't even know if they are still alive but I certainly hope so and doing well.

Chapter 4

So I said good-bye to Houston, loaded up and headed for Nacogdoches. I had pretty much given everything away so one trip is all it took and I was glad because I certainly didn't have the money for another. I had decided to move back to the comforts of home for several reasons, with the main one being that I no longer was in a relationship and Stephen F. Austin had at least a two-to-one ratio of girl-to-boy statistic. I really don't know if that was true, but there were a lot of female type folks walking around on that campus. Another reason... my dad had told me he had a job for me. I would start keeping books and running a tire store for him and would be paid $6.00 per hour for that... how easy was this going to be? Last but not least... I was homesick.

My dad and uncle were opening a tire store in Lufkin and I was going to be the manager...say what? What did I know about tires? I had some on my car... yep, that was about all I knew but it was a job and so into the unknown I ventured. While I worked this tire store, I was able to meet several local police officers. I found out if I made coffee and had donuts... they would come. I befriended a few of Lufkin's finest and enjoyed listening to them talk and tell their war stories. Most of what I heard was bullshit, but every now and then I would get into one of those adventures about law enforcement and actually admire these men and the tales they told. I learned all that one had to do to become a police officer was get hired... back then there was no long academy to go through. It was more of a learn-on-the-job type thing. Hey, this might be for me… oh yes, there was one more thing. You had to be 21 years old and I wasn't yet. So back to my tire store I went and everything was going fairly well right up until the service guy we had hired stole our truck and equipment.

One Monday morning I opened the store and thought, "Sure are a lot of things missing." I found out later that this service man had loaded up everything he could in our truck and "Poof be gone" My uncle and Dad decided that the store wasn't a big money maker so they decided to shut it down. "What now?" says I Again… who came through for me? Yes, you guessed it… my dad. He was going to allow me to work for him in construction at the SFA jobs. Time keeper and errand runner was my official title and for the same pay. How could you beat that?

I was able to get a new dirt bike while doing this tire store stint. I had many in the past and was fairly good at motocross riding. I do have to admit that my dad and I did something during this time that my mother still laughs about now. I had become a pretty good rider and so one weekend I loaded my Suzuki in my dad's truck and took off for Friendswood, Texas and Clover Field Motocross Track. I had never raced competitively and thought it was time to try it. My dad was okay with me racing, but we weren't too sure about my mother.

Years before she had watched me riding at a sand pit area and had to leave when I started making the jumps. It was a great day for me; I placed second in the first heat. I couldn't believe it. The day went on and it was time for the second heat… I was nervous but ready to go. After the dust cleared I was out front and leading the race. That would end soon though… the rider behind me wasn't going to have that and this was the same rider I had chased the whole first race. When the race ended I had a really cool 2nd place trophy.

I did continue to race and my dad continued to support my efforts. Keeping this secret from my mom was going to be easy because she never asked and we never offered. The one thing I didn't think about (now remember, I was so smart) was my mom finding the trophies one day. Lord help us… both of us were in trouble. I do not recall how we made things right but somehow we did and my mother accepted the fact I raced, even though she would not attend one.

The job my dad had waiting started out being sort of easy and I knew it was going to be great. Stay out all night partying and going in to an air-conditioned office just to write down a few things with a possibility of having to go get the bosses something to drink… life was going to be good. Yes sir, I had it made in the shade and remember how smart I was… I could turn this into a goldmine! All that easy way would soon turn on me as more and more responsibilities were handed to me. There were days that I didn't even have time to stop for lunch and on top of all that, I was supposed to get up on walls with the bricklayers and improve my skills whenever I got the chance… What? Wait a minute, what happened to easy?

There was a high point to this though. I was pretty good at being a bricklayer and within a month I was making $7.50 an hour and working on the wall with the others. No more paperwork, no more errands and only eight hours a day. I now had a lot of extra time on my hands and so I decided to take a few classes at SFA and increase my party time too. I'm not sure if that was a wise decision, but it was the one I made and I would never admit I was wrong anyway.

After a few months of this way of life… well… I was tired, wore out and exhausted. From 7:00 am through 3:30 pm, I worked laying brick, then from there I attended one or two classes and lastly, I would go out to a nightclub called Snoopy's until midnight. There were even those nights that an "after hours" party would carry me to daylight and work. I needed to find a way out of this; I was getting old by now… twenty. I had saved a little money and the manager at Snoopy's had offered me a position at the club, so now I had some thinking to do.

I had hooked up with some fraternity guys and was partying with them nearly every night. I was going to go through rush and this fraternity wanted me already but something stopped me… money. Since they wanted some and I didn't have any, it was an easy choice. Those guys were great though because I was able to continue with the partying and some lifetime friendships formed with many of them. As I continued to contemplate my future, I received some news from my dad. The jobs at SFA were coming to an end so he would have to decide if he would return to Houston.

My parents loved it in the country away from the rat race of Houston and after a lot of discussing and scenario playing… they decided to make Nacogdoches their permanent home. Dad would open his own business and my mother could help the office run smooth. I don't know all the details but my folks decided to go into business with a partner. Some man my dad knew from the past; it seemed my dad knew everyone in the Masonry field and they all knew him. They opened an office in Lufkin and started bidding jobs. I, on the other hand, decided to go to work for Snoopy's and stay in school.

I remember my parents being very happy about the decision as they had made some new friends in Nacogdoches. The business was doing well and they bought a new house. I was living with a friend sometimes... then go back home. I did this many times usually when I got low on money. I was attending classes during the day and working at the bar at night... and yes, partying in between and every chance I could get. Nearly everyone that worked at Snoopy's were friends with one another and we spent a lot of time together when not working.

Some of the bartenders lived in a house located on Virginia St. and this became known as Club Virginia. Some of the best nights of those times were spent there. Let's see... I remember there were girls and beer, some music (most everyone played some type of instrument) and then there were girls and beer... and of course girls and beer. There might have even been some of that evil weed known as marijuana also... maybe but I don't remember. The police didn't bother us because we were not in the center of town attracting attention, that and the fact that maybe a few of them were at Club Virginia but again, I don't remember. Poker games could go on for hours at a private lake house owned by a local businessman as well. There were plenty of off-duty police officers showing up and having a good time. I got to know quite a few of the local officers during these days but definitely not all of them.

I was driving to my parent's house one afternoon and got my first ever ticket. I had been up and down the road to their house many times and the speed limit had been lowered to 20 mph due to the road getting a fresh coating of loose gravel. I drove this road often and didn't speed because I didn't want to get a cracked windshield. The normal speed limit was 50 mph, but the road department had placed some temporary signs over the existing ones. When I got on the road this particular day, I noticed the 50 mph were again showing and so I accelerated to 50 mph. There he was, like a cat ready to pounce… a Nacogdoches police officer I had never seen before. He stopped me and told me I was speeding.

He started writing the ticket and I was trying to tell him the signs were down, he just kept writing. I continued to plead my case and told him to just go up the road so he could see the speed limit was 50 again. He finally told me to shut the something up… if I recall it was an ugly word referred to these days as the F-bomb. Hey… I only had to be told once, so I shut the something up as instructed. I'm not for certain if he was just a jerk or that I was just being an obnoxious teenager, but needless to say this was definitely a bad contact experience with the police. I threatened to kick his ass as soon as he drove off too. I was always pretty good at that!

I drove straight to the Police Department, which also housed the Municipal Court. I explained my situation to a very nice lady and she told me she would see if the Judge had time to talk with me. It must have been my day because not only did that Judge have time, he also lived out that road and knew the temporary signs had been removed. The system works and I am proof… or something like that! The Municipal Judge dismissed the ticket and I went on my happy way. I found out a few days later from one of the other officers that my ticket writing buddy was like that to everyone and not to worry about it anymore so I didn't.

One night while I was at Snoopy's, a guy came through the door and he was mad at the world. It was only around 10 pm and we very rarely dealt with drunks until later much less one coming in the door. He was mad at his wife or girlfriend or whatever she was to him and of course she was making the situation worse. Every time we would get him calmed down… she would say something to crank him back up and this continued until he just twisted off and rammed both his fists through the glass front doors of the club. Not just one, but both of them and glass went everywhere. This guy was still standing there with his fists balled up and the employees including me just stood there and stared at this mess. All of sudden, we all started to rush him and one by one he threw us off… what was this guy, Superman?

We continued to rush him and he continued to beat the hell out of us. From the reaction on bystanders' faces, this must have looked like a Bruce Lee movie only with "Shake, shake, shake, shake, shake, shake, shake your booty, shake your bootie" playing in the background. Only if there would have been cell phones with cameras back then… well I'm laughing so hard I can't type. Remember that all the employees were college students and obviously this guy wasn't. After a few more attempts to subdue him, we all sort of backed up because… we were losing! The guy walked off and down the street until he was out of sight. During our failed valiant effort to take this guy down, someone had called the police and within a few minutes three officers arrived.

I didn't know these three officers by sight, but I did know who two of them were by reputation. They walked in the club through the mess and one said, "Somebody broke this glass." Allow me to describe these officers before I go any further. They were all very different… by that I mean one was the shortest cop I'd ever seen, one was a tall lanky kid and the other one (that noticed the broken glass) was "Hoss" from Bonanza. The short one seemed to be calling the shots and let me say, he was feisty. He seemed fearless and confident they would find the guy (remember that his girlfriend or whatever was still there and none of us had thought of that) .The tall lanky one that looked to be maybe twelve years old was sort of just watching and agreeing with the others. Old "Hoss"… well I'm not sure he was all there at all.

He seemed to be interested in something else. Don't misunderstand; he was a nice person, just not really interested in our situation.

Finally, the lady he was mad at stepped forward and told the short one her name and the guy's name. She told him where they lived and explained to him what had happened earlier that brought this situation to this level. She pleaded for the officers to not hurt him and she could go calm him down for them. The shorter officer was not afraid at all and was bouncing around like a bandy rooster ready for action while the tall lanky one agreed. Old "Hoss", well I don't think cared one way or the other. As she continued with her story all of a sudden she told those officers he was an ex Green Beret and had served in Vietnam. What the hell… we just got whipped by Billy Jack. I saw the movies, was he the real life version? The shorter officer didn't seem fazed at all and in a few minutes the three officers and the lady left.

Don't know how that ended, but it sure gave the employees something to talk about… "He better be glad he left when he did!" Little did I know that that short feisty officer would one day be my boss and later a friend. As for that tall lanky one… he would become one of the best friends I ever had, but I will talk about them later.

Day in and day out, I would attend class and every night except Sunday I would be at Snoopy's until closing and beyond. I had several girlfriends, some of them waitresses and some students at the college that I attempted to shuffle from one another. That didn't work too well and I always seemed to be at odds with some of them, but hey, this was college and it is supposed to be this way... right? I guess the only real problem I had at the time was not enough time... I was getting old, remember I was twenty. I guess I thought that this era would last forever but the days started crawling along and I was becoming less interested in, well, everything.

I found myself more interested in getting out in the world and starting a normal life. I was listening to some new guy named George Straight... this wasn't rock and roll but it was new and I was sick of the disco crap. What? Me, Mr. Rock and Roll listening to country music... say it ain't so. My interest started to center on one girl... I must be contracting a terrible disease...! My whole way of thinking was slowly changing, but, it was okay. I began seeing that one girl a lot. She was a local girl working at the local newspaper and within a few months we started talking about marriage. I actually started watching the news on television and picking up something more than Penthouse or Playboy to "read"... the newspaper became interesting. I started thinking about all types of different things and was trying things I thought were not cool before. My choice in clothes went back to Levi's and flannel shirts... even the old desert boots came back. I wanted to trade my mustang in on a pickup... a pickup? That's what all the Goat Ropers and Shit Kickers drove, why did I want one? My motorcycle started collecting dust and the last time I rode it was to pick up this new girlfriend at her parent's house, another brilliant idea I might say.

When this new girl and I started seeing each other, I had a car and of course... a motorcycle. One day I was going to pick her up from her house and decided to ride the motorcycle. I did not know her parents very well at all but what the heck, everyone loved motorcycles. It was a beautiful day and I had an extra helmet (it was law then to wear a helmet) When I arrived I was greeted with the worst stares one could imagine. Her dad was shaking his head no and her mom had her hands up on her face with that "Oh No" look. There I was in all my glory, long hair still and on a motorcycle to take their daughter. They must have thought I was a 1% biker gang member the way the stares were beaming at me, and the words were all similar... "No way, no way... not my daughter." I was given the daddy's little girl speech and advised that the cargo was too precious to allow her on the back of that evil machine I had arrived on.

I guess I would have understood better if it was a black chopper with skulls all over it but it was a gold and white Yamaha 650. The four of us stood there and were joined by her little brother who immediately said, "Cool" as we discussed the options now being offered to me. Do you have a car? Can you ride your motorcycle back to town and get your car? Even though that was a twenty-five mile round trip it was the one her daddy favored. And... the discussion went on for a while before her mother decided that I wasn't so bad after all and if I would be real careful and bring her home in my car it would be okay. It probably took an hour to get permission to take her on my bike. It all worked out though, we made it safely, switched over to my car as promised and got her home that evening in one piece.

Chapter 5

By now things were really changing and in a hurry too. I knew I couldn't work the club anymore if I was about to start building a future so I again went to my dad and told him I needed a good job… and guess what? Yep, I was going back to work as a bricklayer for him while learning to be a foreman and estimator. I'm not real sure I knew what that meant at the time but the money was good, the hours seemed right and so you know what I did? Bought a new truck and got right back in debt. Oh, but this wasn't just a truck, it was a full time four-wheel drive, short wheel base, lifted up truck with big tires and a 400 engine. Pretty blue and light blue combination, aluminum spoke wheels, a winch and best of all… got about 8 miles to the gallon truck. Wow… I was riding in style now.

I was riding in style so much that I had to move back in with my parents to save up some money. Yeah… by now we had decided to get married. Let me explain that before I made this decision to work for my Dad, I actually went to the Police Department and asked about going to work… must be 21, well I was not quite, but to seal the deal I found out what an officer made (choke choke) Are you kidding me? I would have to take a cut in pay to go to work with the police and wait a few months to boot. Now you know. She was working, I was working and everything was starting to gel just right. Time to set a date and find a place to live and that is just what we did.

We were building a bank account together, looking at apartments along with all the furnishings and household goods needed to start a new home. It seemed we had put everything in motion and she would work forever at The Daily Sentinel and I would be in the masonry business and we would live happily ever after. Well… that's not exactly how the story went as we faced the same problems all people face. We did get a nice apartment, small, but nice. One bedroom and one combo living/kitchen/dining room and a small bathroom down stairs under some college students. We decided on a wedding in November and now the wait started.

We were both 20 years old but I was almost 21 and still was very smart… remember? The days went by fast and finally we were only a week away from the wedding. She had all her friends for bridesmaids and I had… well I had a collection of friends that had absolutely nothing in common with each other. Two of them were cousins but different as night and day. We had a good time but must have looked like the FIVE Stooges. That would be Larry, Curly , Moe, Shemp and Butthead. As the ceremony was starting, two of my friends came walking up the backside of the church right past the alter area. At least there was comedy entertainment as they attempted to get to a seat without being noticed. By the way, I had turned 21 by this time, but the idea of going to work for less money as a police officer didn't appeal to me. I was still thinking about that River Oaks Mansion only in Nacogdoches. I pretty much placed being a police officer on the back shelf and was ready to start being grown… right.

Things started out really well for us, between our parents we had everything we needed to get a life together up and going. The wedding went well with no problems but we didn't have a lot of extra money to spend, so a few days in Hot Springs, Arkansas would have to do as a honeymoon. I don't think it really mattered anyway; we were on our own and at this time, didn't have a worry in the world. After the return to Nacogdoches we made our home in the apartment and both went to our jobs. This is what you do… right? We started to save up some money because we found out very quickly that this little apartment wasn't going to be big enough for very long. After several months an opportunity was presented to us that was just too good to pass on.

The owner of five duplexes located in the middle of town had offered us the management position of this complex. We paid a reduced amount of rent and all we had to do was keep the place looking good. Wow… what a start, this would be easy and we would have extra money. Well, with all my wisdom that extra money meant a bass boat and that's exactly what we bought (like we needed a boat). Her parents had a very nice ski boat that we could use for free anytime we wanted but… I wanted one for fishing and came up with any reason I could to purchase this boat. And did I mention we had purchased her a newer car? The one she had was fine but we had to have another one, fancier and a different color than green. I guess we liked those monthly payments because we kept adding them to our monthly responsibilities. So things rocked on while at the duplex and we would make that our home for a while.

Life was good and we were accumulating necessities as well as luxuries. We had a group of friends that we did something with nearly every weekend. There was always a party somewhere and we didn't miss one. Do you remember that tall lanky officer from Snoopy's? He was part of the group and he constantly told me his war stories which increased my desire to be and officer. But I would put that on hold for now, the money coming was too good and we had dreams to fulfill.

The day came along that we started looking for a house to buy and some of our friends were into real estate so… we got the call that the perfect starter home was about to be on the market. It really was too, it had everything we wanted. There were three bedrooms and two baths, two car garage, fireplace and only about a year old. It was sitting in a new up-and- coming neighborhood and best of all, we could afford it. My pay had increased rather well and taking on a house payment wasn't going to hurt us. All we had to do was come up with six thousand dollars and so we made an offer on this perfect little house.

I never will forget the day our friend called us at home to let us know the status of our offer. We were both home from work and watching the "Ehhhhh" and "Woah" of the Fonze when we learned that the owners had accepted the offer. Damn… we were about to be home owners ourselves! By now our income was rather nice especially for people our age and after waiting for all the paperwork and inspections and anything else that was thrown at us, we had a house and now it was time to personalize it. A little new furniture, some fencing, few boards here and there, and oh yeah… a baby bed! We had found out we were going to be parents just before buying the house. I will never forget the day I came in from work to my wife shaking her head yes and seeing baby stuff from the doctor on the table. It was time to let the folks know and I don't know that I had seen a happier bunch of people ever. I am not sure if I was feeling happiness or just fear, but it was a good feeling and I loved it.

There are a few problems that came along though, such as more money meant more hours. More hours meant… away from home.

By this time my dad had broken free form his partner and started his own masonry company, called it Tri-City Masonry. He decided that we would only do commercial and extremely large residential work. His reputation opened many doors with the local contractors and he was also bidding work outside the immediate area.

There was something really cool about this new business... on the business card it read; Tri –City Masonry, P.O.Box 104, Nacogdoches, Texas, Nacogdoches- Lufkin- Your City, My dad's name, President, my name, Vice President. I was the VP of the company and that also came with a raise. Nobody ever told me but I feel I got this because of the grandkid headed our way. With good always comes a little bad and running the out of town jobs was mine. Every job that was out of Nacogdoches at a distance too far to drive everyday was mine to run. We rented an apartment, used travel trailers... whatever it took. Cell phones still didn't exist to the public so this sometimes was very difficult on a couple expecting their first child. As tensions grew around the house, the money seemed to make it all better. I made more in the 80's than I do now.

My parents had built a new house outside of the city and we bought the property that backed up to theirs. We started thinking about building a larger home because... just three years after the first baby, it was number two's turn to show up. I was working on a job nearly three hours from home when the second baby came along. I got home in time to go to the hospital and the following week had to be back out of town. Bear in mind that my wife was still working at the newspaper as well.

Before I get too far ahead let me back up for a low moment in our life... my wife and I both had younger brothers. Her brother and my youngest brother were friends and did a few things together.

For example, one night her brother got into a fight and even though he won, he was swollen and a little bloody and bruised. My brother brought him to our house for full repairs before he showed up at home. On the other hand he came with my little brother when we loaned my brother our car and someone hit it... so they basically tag teamed us with things they got in to. We always helped them out just because. Her little brother went off to Texas A&M to get his degree and seemed to be doing real well.

He was a bright young man, strong as a bull and would work all day long if needed. That dreadful night... oh how I remember it, just like it happened yesterday. I was getting ready to go on a fishing trip and my wife was cleaning up the kitchen. We had just put number one in bed and we got a call. Her brother had been injured in an accident in College Station and her parents were on the way there. Shortly after that the doorbell chimed and when I opened the door my wife took one look and collapsed to the ground.

It was our preacher and people from the church. Her brother had passed away from his injuries. Just 19 years old and he was gone. I don't think she ever recovered from that even through today. I saw my father-n-law weep and that caused me to do the same. I asked over and over again... Why? Maybe I've never gotten over it either. I know all families go through tragic times but we really struggled with this. It took a very long time to even talk about it among ourselves. As the days went by though and so much happening in our lives, we must have placed it aside so we could move forward. He was just so young with such a bright future.

Our second child came along later on and we continued to move on. The new house was under construction and was going to be nice, twice the size of our present one. We acted as contractors so there were many long nights spent out at the site while my wife was home tending to the kids. But… every now and then she found a way to come out and sometimes brought the little ones. There were no out of town jobs at the time so being able to finish up the new house was so much easier. We worked and worked and everybody in both families worked until our new house was complete. And one day, we were moved in and ready for a break.

So… with six other friends we booked a trip to Jamaica. Yep… left the boys with my parents and off to Houston to get on the plane headed south! What a trip… best part of the flight is when I won the drawing. Everyone on the plane wrote their seat number on a one dollar bill and placed it in a bag… drew my seat number. Over two hundred extra dollars to spend but all in ones. Remember that tall, lanky officer again? He was among the eight friends that made the trip. Only thing was now he was no longer an officer or detective because he had started his own P.I. business although in its infancy… he was doing well. That was one of the most fun trips ever and only our kiddos made us want to come home. I do have a funny story about my buddy and I and it took place on a rainy day down there in Negril, Jamaica.

We stayed at Hedonism II resort for adults. We knew it would be fun when we saw the advertisement poster for the place. If you've ever seen it you know what I'm talking about… the Mona Lisa with a boob hanging out! Anyway… there was a ping pong table in one of the pavilions and my buddy was pretty good at the game. He was holding the table and none of the challengers weren't able to defeat him. Two very attractive girls from New Jersey walked in wearing something resembling bikini's about three sizes too small. One of the girls challenged my buddy and so it began. At one point, he hit the ball back short and she had to lean way over the table to return it.

My eyes must have popped out of my head but I didn't think anyone noticed. By the end of the match, my buddy won and I looked around to find a dozen guys back there looking at what I was looking at. We laughed at that for hours and swore to everyone back home that had to have been Miss New Jersey. That trip did a lot of good for us by easing the stress we were feeling from more out of town work. We made a few diving trips while there, ate some fantastic food, drank all we could and even tried something called "Special Cake."

This cake was a deep chocolate cake laced with ganja (marijuana) and didn't know it until after we ate it… what a crazy night that was but I don't remember. So on to the plane to take us back to our boys and our home. It didn't take long for the same old grind to set in… out of town jobs were getting to me. I needed to be with my family, I needed to be at home when nighttime came. One day out of the blue, my dad ask me if I would be interested in doing the office work, you know job take offs and bidding with the contractors. I had learned how to do this over the years but never used it.

I decided that this may be the only way to be at home every now and then. I also had been using a little of my education and was doing drafting designs blueprints for homes. I actually had a pretty good side business going there for a while… designed and drafted up several homes and small commercial buildings in the area. I would take the drawings to a local business that had a blueprint machine and they made everything look nice and professional. Everything kept moving along and honestly our income wasn't too shabby at all. My wife had started to move up the corporate ladder and was making good money… only one thing though, we were spending a lot of that money on "Grownup toys" and things we didn't need. The kids, number one and number two were growing. We were getting to take them places like Six Flags, Sea World and Fiesta Texas. We made all sorts of short family trips and had a ball doing it. There is one thing that I regret not doing with them… going to Disney World.

While all of this work was going on, well you know the saying, "What goes up must come down"? I noticed that there were fewer and fewer jobs to bid. The bigger jobs we desired were further and further away from home. We employed many people and at one time, nearly a hundred. We had enough equipment to supply several different jobs at one time, in other words our overhead was high. We didn't have anything we didn't need but to keep up with several construction jobs all at once required a lot of equipment and ways to move that equipment. The job market continued to dry up and we had no choice but to downsize the company. We had full time salaried people we kept as long as possible. One of these people was an equipment mechanic, really good and very loyal to my dad.

My dad was trying to think of something to supplement the business and having this mechanic available seemed like the key to that situation. We could take in small repair work to keep him busy during down times. We found a building on the west loop of Nacogdoches and it was perfect. Nice office area for the masonry business and a large shop for repairing our equipment along with any others. There was a parts room, a break type room, a showroom and of course two bathrooms all on a couple of acres. We made the decision to purchase it and after a little remodeling and a few fences, we were ready to go as Tri-City Masonry and H&H Tractor and Repair.

We brought in a line of lawn mowers, chain saws, weed eaters and other things that would sell on sight. We took on oil products and lubricants, hardware and lots of other handy items. There was even a line of farm implements brought in. We hired the mechanics brother to run the sales and service department to begin with. I was splitting my time with both companies and looking back now was stretched way too thin. The business had fair success but at times seemed to do really well. We decided to expand and took on a tractor line, Massey Ferguson. Things got real busy for a while with the out of town jobs, some as far away as 150 miles, going on and the sales and service at the tractor store beginning to take off.

Businesses running, kids growing and life looked good except for the fact that I was again never home. As the saying goes… Places to go, people to see and things to do were again interfering with my family time. Trouble started brewing around the house and a once great relationship started to unwind but very slowly. Sometime during this period the construction jobs began drying up again. When I say that I mean came to a halt. With only one job left to finish and it was in Texarkana, Texas and to go along with that… general sales were down as well. Interest rates had soared and financing anything was terrible and we were not selling enough to pay the bills anymore.

The business was in its infancy and sales just stopped. We managed to keep the doors open a little longer by cashing in CD's and personal loans but no matter… we no longer had the capital to keep it going. We did manage to retain some of our investment by selling off the owned equipment, fixtures and finally the building. All in all it was a terrible loss and just a waste of two years of time and worry. We weren't broke and had funds to continue on but I was sure worn out. The economy as many of you can remember took several more years to recover and so this early closing may have just been a blessing in disguise.

My parents sold their home and moved into a small lake house they had bought and my dad started hunting for jobs to bid. This one job in Texarkana wasn't going to last forever. We found a travel trailer and set it up in Texarkana so I could stay there and finish up that job. Again... I was away from my family for a week at a time. I realize that people do this all the time but I could never get used to it and was really miserable the entire time I was away. After all, I missed a major part of my boys' lives and placed the entire task of raising kids on my wife while she maintained a full time job. When I did come in on the weekends, it would be 7:00 or 8:00 Friday night before I got there and I would leave Sunday afternoon to go back. So not only was raising the kids all hers, so was... well... everything. I didn't know it yet but a new way of life was about to be available for me to choose.

Chapter 6

There were several things I could always count on… one was I could make a living with masonry; two, I had the best and most loyal friends ever. This would start out being the strangest few months to date as best I remember. The Texarkana job was winding down to nothing and there were no other jobs in the near future. A large masonry company out of Houston had offered my dad a job with a healthy salary and he was thinking about trying it. He spoke with me about going on this job with him and my pay would be really good as well, just one catch… it was on the east coast in Virginia. Talk about raising some discussions around our houses and loud ones too. My folks decided to buy a fifth-wheel travel trailer and give it a try… sort of a travel and work thing. I don't know if my mother really wanted to go but she did in support of my dad.

When I asked my wife she flat out stated that if I went, I would go alone (PERIOD) I wasn't ready for that, I truly loved my family and did not want to leave them here but that wasn't going to happen so… for the first time in my life I told my dad "No". He understood and started pulling equipment to my barn for me to keep in Texas and be able to do small jobs.

He and my mother stayed in Texas a few weeks and during this time, he helped me gather a few houses to brick along with some small repair type work. I had about six weeks back logged and was bidding more every day. I was keeping myself, four bricklayers and helpers busy but not really making more than wages... it was just that way in East Texas at that time. A fireplace here a fence there and repairs inside existing buildings were on the menu but we did stay busy. Remember that tall lanky officer turned P.I.? He had gotten me to help him on some of his surveillance work and not only was it fun, it started me back wanting to be in law enforcement. At 31 years old I was getting awful tired of scratching a living off of a mortar board. Time moved on and kids grew only now number one was in school and so was number 2... I missed their childhood and I regret that even today. I missed so much, but I thought I was doing well. My wife and I gave them everything they could ever want. Or did we? I still wonder about that today. So what was there? I was at my crossroads and was about the most miserable person ever... well probably not ever but I wasn't happy.

My wife was still there and my friends all were still there and surely something would come along soon. Some of those friends were police officers, detectives and one was the Chief of Police himself. Not only was he the chief, he was a great person and friend. Remember that new way of life I talked about? Lots of discussion, planning and promising... and maybe even a little begging, my wife and I would sell our house and move into a less expensive one. Not only that, we sold all of our toys including some vehicles, a boat, some ATV's and a lot more... all for a good reason... I was going to enroll in the Police Academy.

My parents were in Virginia now and my youngest brother had followed to go to work. My other brother remained in Nacogdoches and would land a job with the City Street Department and then the Housing Authority. My sister-n- law would help create O'Malley's

Alley Cats due to her love of animals and I was back in a classroom about to fulfill a long time dream. This was going to be the perfect year if only I could pass this academy.

Writing about my friends brings back many really good memories that I would like to share. Most of them revolve around a 108 acre piece of property we called the Deer Lease. It really wasn't a lease, my wife's grandmother owned it and we hunted and rode ATVs there for years. My tall, lanky friend was probably the worst hunter; ever even though he believed he was an American hunting legend. No patience at all were his downfall and he provided us with many laughable moments. I remember on one weekend while we were at the lease, he was going to the woods to kill a deer and that is all he talked about the night before while we camped. Up bright and early with his Browning gear on (from head to toe, all Browning) he started his adventure. The boots he wore were very noisy and he could be heard a long ways off only he didn't travel very far then he stopped. Oh well, maybe he went down in the creek bed. The other friend, a local banker, took off for his stand and I decided to stay at camp and drink coffee while they froze in those deer stands.

Our camp was an unused hay barn that we had converted into a make shift cabin. We had enclosed most of it, put a wood burning stove in it, tents acted like bedrooms and some old carpet made a floor you could walk on in your socks. There was two Coleman cooktop stoves set on a makeshift cabinet and an air tight container for keeping food in. We even put a door on it to keep the critters out at night. Outside we had a fire pit with a tripod cooking stand and plenty of chairs for hanging out around the fire. It was great and we all loved going there year round. Anyway, everyone had left the camp except me and I was sitting on a stand inside the barn (basically a ladder and about a six foot opening in the top of a side wall) that allowed a look at the entire upper pasture area. I didn't have a gun, only field glasses and I was scanning the woods just to see what I could find. It was getting daylight and I saw something moving so I focused in and it was my tall, lanky buddy sitting at the top of an old lean type stand about eight feet off the ground.

He was only about sixty yards from me but a small patch of woods kept him invisible unless a person had binoculars and I did! I continued to watch the area scanning back to him every few minutes because he was moving around so much. He would raise and lower his head apparently to try to see something, reminded me of a turkey, it was funny with the looks on his face and all. I kept scanning and then I saw it... a small young buck with three points about the size of my fingers. Surely this isn't what the Great Hunter is looking at... is it? Turns out, it was and now I was watching the little buck and my friend to see what the outcome of this encounter would be. The two were only about thirty yards apart and my buddy finally saw the deer. I watched through my binoculars as he raised his rifle and waited to hear the report ... and waited, and waited, and waited. Scanning over to the deer it almost appeared they had a stare off going on.

While I was watching the deer... BOOM! He pulled the trigger and the little deer jumped and hopped off into some trees. I swung the binoculars back and what did I see? My friend, my buddy must have forgotten he was about eight feet off the ground because he stepped off the stand. Yes sir... to ground but landed on his feet with rifle in tow. The look on his face told me he was in pain but he gathered himself and started running towards the deer. He stumbled around for a while and I saw he was now walking towards the camp so I poured a cup of coffee for him and waited. He showed up a few minutes later and was limping. I, holding back my laughter, asked him was that him that shot and he replied, "Yeah, but I think I hit this huge buck. He must have gotten away."

I asked about his limp and he replied, "I was chasing him and must have tripped over something; my knees are hurting." Holding back my laughter was really hard but I controlled it. I am so proud that I did because by now our other friend had returned from his stand because he was too cold and needed some hot coffee. The three of us sat around the stove, drank our coffee and my tall, lanky friend told us about the huge deer. This was a wall hanger for sure. I finally told them that we needed to go find that deer. My tall, lanky buddy was a little reluctant but agreed to go look, so out of the camp and into the woods we went in search of the huge deer. The three of us wandered around in the area and our banker friend located some blood... he had hit it! I was looking and noticed my tall, lanky buddy was kicking leaves around.

I just stared laughing and yelled over at him "Well, you're not going to find him under those leaves." His reply was rather vulgar and I vowed not to use the f-bomb in this story. Eventually we found the deer sort of in a low area and when Ol' tall and lanky saw the antlers he was speechless. Banker man asked if that was the deer and after a few moments he replied, "There must have more deer with him. I must have shot this by accident. It will make good camp meat anyway." And so ends one of the many Great Hunter stories... I sure miss those days.

On another weekend at the deer lease, both number one and number two were with us. Let's see there was... Banker buddy, Chief buddy, Marine buddy, number one and two along with Chief buddy's son-n-law and I all together for the weekend. What a fun weekend it was even though Chief buddy was the only one with a successful hunt. We cooked out in the open area because the weather was gorgeous and told tall tales and probably had an adult beverage or two. Everyone hated to leave that Sunday evening but work waited Monday morning. I pulled in at our house and my wife had supper ready for all of us... yep, chicken fried deer steaks.

The table was set and the meal looked delicious... a perfect ending to a perfect weekend... right? Wrong! Number two was eating away and finished the deer steak on his plate; his mom asked if he wanted her to cut him up some more meat. Oh my goodness, the words that came out of his mouth still haunt me today. He looked up at his mom and said "I can get my own (f-bomb)ing meat, thank you very much"

My head dropped and I could feel her X-ray vision burning a hole through my scalp. Number two went on eating while his mom explained to him what was wrong with what he said. My scolding would come later. Seems he learned a lot at the deer lease and she let all the buddies know about this too! Just one more and I will stop on the deer lease; it was such a great place and full of wonderful memories with family and friends, I can't help but one more.

Seems we were up at the deer lease every weekend for years and made it up most holidays as well. One such trip had Ol' tall and lanky, Marine buddy and me at the camp. We arrived on a Friday afternoon and set up everything... then started to make up some supper. I do not recall what we cooked but after eating and drinking a few adult beverages we all decided to serious hunt the following morning. When morning came, it was cold, I mean cold! I chickened out and told them I was staying in the camp with the fire and hot coffee. Both of them decided to brave the cold and hit the woods.

It must have taken them thirty minutes to put all those clothes on but finally they were ready to head out. While drinking their last cup of coffee, I was getting teased about being cold. They both laughed at me, called me some insulting names and Ol' tall and lanky gave me some Great Hunter advice. "You ain't going to kill a deer sitting in the barn." I had to come back with something so I popped off that when he heard my rifle at 9 o'clock, he should start back this way to help drag the deer to the camp. I planned to shoot the rifle at 9:00 just to mess with him. Again with insulting names and making fun of me and the cold, they left out right before daylight. It had started snowing and sleeting and the wind began to blow harder. I stayed close to the wood stove for a while and as it began to lighten up, I got up on my camp stand to watch the snow accumulate. It was an overcast day but really pretty as the ground started turning white.

I got up and down several times, smoked cigarettes and made all kinds of noises because I wasn't expecting to see anything. A couple of times I was on the stand I didn't even have a gun with me. It was getting pretty light outside, so for some reason I got back on the stand and took a rifle this time. As I sat there, I thought about how cold them other two were and got tickled about it. I reached down and turned on some Willie Nelson and was just looking at the white cover everything. After a few minutes, I saw some movement and thought it might be one of my friends returning. Neither had gone in that direction but with Ol' tall and lanky... you never knew.

After a few more minutes I could tell it was a lone deer headed right towards the camp. I couldn't tell if it was a buck or a doe so I just kept watching until it exited the wood line... a large buck with a large rack. What the... this was a nice deer, maybe not a Boone & Crockett, but a nice East Texas buck. Looking through my scope I could count nine points. As I watched him enter the open area, for some reason I looked at my watch and it was about one minute until 9:00... Really? What kind of luck was this, were the Deer Hunting Gods looking down on me?

I thought about what I had said to 'Ol tall and lanky and an evil grin must have come over my face like never before. So here I am, looking through a scope, then at my watch, back and forth until the watch showed 9:00 and... BOOM! That deer dropped where it stood while my heart was racing 100 mph. All you hunters will know what that feels like. The woods were quiet for only a second when I heard Ol' tall and lanky yell, "_ _ _ _ you asshole." I believe it was that f-bomb again.

And so the wait began for my friends to walk out of the woods. Marine buddy showed up first and was laughing about me shooting at 9 o'clock. I pointed and handed him the binoculars and told him he was not going to believe what happened. Once he saw the deer he damn near cried, laughing so hard. We both continued to wait for Ol' tall and lanky to show up and within a half hour we heard the "clop,clop,clop" of those Browning boots he wore. He was cursing, calling me everything in the book when he got to the barn he said, "Very funny, asshole. I had a huge deer in my sights ready to shoot... and your shot scared him off"

He continued to rant and rave while Marine buddy was grinning from ear to ear. He finally asked Marine buddy what he thought was so funny about him losing a deer because of all the shooting (one shot) going on... Marine buddy just broke out laughing. I turned towards him because I could not look him in the face without breaking up and said "When you stop your bitching, I need help dragging my deer to the barn". That could never happen again but it happened that day. I still tell that story with Marine buddy all the time... good times they were.

Anyway, back to the Police Academy... it was about to start and I was ready, but at the same time a little nervous. Hadn't been in a classroom for a while and I was concerned about how I would react. So the day finally came for me to report for the academy and I pulled into the parking lot to see a gentleman in slacks, starched shirt and a tie on standing in front of the building. He was flipping his tie similar to the way W.C. Fields did in his movies and smiling. I remember as I entered the parking lot, the bottom of my car hit. I was driving my '82 Vette with maybe a couple of inches ground clearance. When I walked to the door of the building this man said, "Bad entrance for such a nice car. Do you want to sell that thing?" I told him no but if I decided to, I would let him know. He regularly asked if I was ready to sell but I wasn't. Later I would learn this man was going to be my main instructor at the academy.

Everyone gathered in the large meeting room turned classroom and as we all had coffee and... shall I say it? Yes... donuts, he started to meet and greet everybody. A friendly man with a dry sense of humor and a constant smile (more like a shit eating grin) asked us to take a seat. We all chose a seat and he started explaining what was to be expected from us as students and what we could expect from him as a teacher. I sort of liked the way he conducted himself, even though I could tell he could be a hard-ass if he wanted... after all he was also a police officer.

His expectations were not that difficult as he only wanted for the students or cadets to pay attention to the instructors, participate in the drills and pass all the tests. And… there were a lot of tests. First of all there would be a spelling test every Monday morning, including this one… get out a sheet of paper. If we were going to write reports we better damn sure know how to spell the law enforcement words and terms. There would also be a test every Friday at the end of that week's training. And on top of that… a final two hundred question test before you were allowed to take the two hundred question State test. There was one little, small, tiny detail left… you could not fail any of them (even spelling) or you would be asked to leave. OK… no problem… right? Let the games begin… this is what I had waited for and I was in it 100 percent.

The academy was very different from regular school or college classes. There was no warming up to anything… it was jump in with both feet on everything. Work your ass off for an hour or so then take a short refreshment and bathroom break then back to work. Everything was moving really fast and you could tell at the end of the first week which students were going to excel and which ones were not. I chose to be one that would and did what I had to do to learn the material. Then came the first weeks test… what was this? I walked right through it; I knew the answers to the questions. It was like I had been doing this forever and the score is 100. There was only one other student that received that score and the competition started!

Chapter 7

Week two was pretty much a carbon copy of week one… a spelling test and then lots of intense classroom instruction. Now I will tell you that by the second week this instructor had loosened up a bit as well as most of the students so there were times that some jokes and war stories were told. So even though the work was a heavy load, the days seemed to go by a little smoother with a little comedy relief. The second week test… another 100. That other student, well he received a 100 as well and we were still neck and neck.

Then came week three and the code of criminal procedure… a little harder subject and if I remember correctly; final score 95 to 95. Week four and the hardest week of them all or so the instructor told us, Penal Code. This was the nut cruncher, this was the terminator, and this was the week that would thin the class down… crap! Lots of numbers to match to lots of laws, memory, memory, memory and I sweated it all week long. If I didn't pass this test what was I going to tell my wife? What was I going to tell myself? Friday arrived right on time and as he distributed the tests you could see the worry on everyone's faces, you could feel the tension in the air… you could… wait a minute, I read the first question and I knew the answer. Then the second one… same thing, what the hell? I would finish up the test and even though I did get a little confused on a couple of questions… score 90. One problem though, that other guy scored a 92 and now I was in second place but not by far.

So each week the instructions and material continued to pour in and the Friday test would always arrive. 100 to 100 week after week until firearm week. The most fun week of them all... shooting at the range and a little classroom work that went with it. We were to shoot daytime and nighttime and qualify at the end of the week. We were to shoot shotguns and handguns... the handgun would be a service revolver with a 4 inch barrel. I had my Colt King Cobra and had been shooting it a long time... needless to say I felt comfortable with it but would have preferred my 1911 .45. We shot targets in the daylight, we shot targets at night and of course we took a test both at the range and in the class.

At the end of the day I had evened the score. This other student and I were not against each other; we had become friends but the competition was fun and thinking back, probably what kept both of us focused. The instructor started of every new week with an update on the rivalry and then hit us with our spelling test. The weeks moved on and we moved into traffic stops. Another fun week... party time, paintball gun style! I knew the management at the local Expo Center due to the fact my wife and I headed up a benefit BBQ every year for the Foster Parents/Kids Association.

A quick little history; It was called the Do Dat Barbeque and put on every September in Nacogdoches. My wife and a co-worker put the very first one together. About 15 cook teams showed up. There was a cover charge at the gate and not only did the teams compete in different categories they offered samples to the attendees. Free beer for those of age was supplied by local distributors so the turnout was good. I became involved the following year and honestly enjoyed every minute of this benefit. The best part... seeing the money go to the kids in need.

This event grew to over a hundred teams in the sixteen years that my wife and I controlled it. We had the best support and help one could ever ask for and distributed somewhere around $500,000.00 into our community in those years. Loved every minute of it! Now back to the Expo Center... I was stating that I knew the management and we were allowed to use the covered show barn for our exercises. Good thing too because it rained a lot that week!

The instructors had set up scenarios where two officers would make a traffic stop. They had other students play the offender parts after they went through their turn. They also brought in seasoned officers to play the offender parts. The scenarios ranged from a normal... did I say normal? There is no such thing as a normal traffic stop! They ranged from a stop where nothing unusual happened to a stop where the offender takes shots at the officer. All day for a couple of days we made stop after stop. The story goes... win some, lose some, and I don't believe a single student got through that exercise without being hit by a paintball a couple of times.

We even had one smartass that placed his paintballs in an ice chest... if you've ever been hit by a paintball then you know it stings... right? Get hit by one that has been on ice and is hardened and it hurts like hell. Well, what goes around... comes around, so I don't need to tell you how the end to this problem came about. All and all, it was a blast but also eye opening because it taught you just how fast a stop could go bad and most of all, just how fast an officer can be shot performing a traffic stop. Again the written test came along and the score was 100 to 100.

The twelve weeks were winding down and all of the students had become a close group, including the instructors involved. We started finishing up and then the last week was upon us before we realized the academy was about to be over. This family we had become was about to all go their separate ways. One of the students and I were already hired by the Nacogdoches Police Department providing we pass the state test. That was a day to remember… the assistant Chief of Police showed up one day while we were in class and talked for a while then, called another student and myself outside. He told us that the department had made a decision to hire the two of us with one stipulation… we pass the state test on the first try.

Several other students had offers from the Lufkin Police Department and a couple of county agencies. Texas Forrest Service offered one and anyway there were several. The first few days were spent reviewing for the class final exam and we were told that would help on the state test as well. Everyone took these days very seriously… remember you could not fail a single test. Thursday morning arrived and here was our schedule; we would do one last review in the morning hours, and then take the final test in the afternoon. On Friday we would gather at an auditorium on SFA campus for graduation and then after lunch we would take the state test. Later that night we were having a big party at a rented hall on the loop. Pretty hectic scheduling for just a few days.

The review started and the instructor was throwing everything at us trying to get all the students ready. He dismissed us for lunch and most of the students stayed at the building to get a little extra studying in. After lunch, all the tables were cleared off and he began passing out the tests. Lots of questions but they were all multiple choice answers. I received mine and began to read the questions… number one, that was easy, number two, again easy. Down the page I went and didn't look around to see anyone and what they were

60

doing. Finally number two hundred, got it! I only had a problem with a couple of questions throughout the entire test.

When I was finished I looked up and everyone else was still working but in a few minutes my competition was also finished. We looked at one another, smiled and took our papers up to the front before we stepped outside to wait for the rest to finish up. There was a two or three hour limit (Don't remember which one) and we were through in an hour. He and I sat around outside for a good while before others started out. When the time frame ended there were still a few that had not completed the questions. We waited for the results and it was a little nerve racking even though I knew I had passed.

I felt good about the results and if there would have been cell phones, then I would have called everyone in my family. The grades finally came out and we all went back inside to see our results. When I saw my paper and 99.5 on the top, I couldn't believe it. I had only missed one question! I looked to my competition and he told me 99.5 as well. We had tied; we had the same average and were in fact the Co-Valedictorians of the academy. All the hard work had paid off now the state test awaited. As far as the others, I believe every single student passed the final but some not by much. It was a great feeling to go home with that news... my wife was excited and we went out to eat for a celebration.

Friday morning and time to get ready to graduate... oh yeah, and take the state test too. I was ready and I didn't do any more studying because if I didn't know it by now, I wasn't going to learn it in a few more minutes. Everyone and their family members started arriving at the auditorium and it filled up quickly. The speakers began and made the announcement about the race for valedictorian... my mother and father-n-law were really happy about that, hell I was too.

The ceremony was simple and relatively short and the head of the academy thanked everyone for attending then advised for the students to return at 1:00 pm for the state exam. My family went to lunch and I relaxed as much as I could and like I mentioned, I was through studying. I was ready for the test.

I remember thinking that maybe I was meant to be a police officer... not only had I completed the academy on top of the class, I had a lot of fun doing it. I never regretted signing up and investing money in it. I was a happy person. The only thing wrong right now was my mom and dad, along with my youngest brother were in Virginia and I missed them terribly. I recall the phone conversation with them regarding my grades and how proud my dad sounded when he heard the news. I think he knew all along that I wasn't supposed to be in the construction business even though at one time it was our plan to be there together. I think he knew some other things as well but we will get into that later. So... time was closing in on the state test and before I knew it I was headed for SFA to take it on.

I entered a large classroom in one of the buildings and there were typical college desks... you know the type that look like a chair with a small writing platform on them? We were seated so that everyone had an empty desk all the way around them. I guess so no one would cheat, although at this level, I didn't think that would be necessary. We were given a Scan-Tron type answer sheet and had several pencils at each desk. I can only assume that the state has far different testing rules than the rest of the agencies but whatever... bring me the questions. Then came all the warnings and the three hour time limit (to the second) and finally they began handing out the booklets. There were no associates of the academy in the room, only state people... and us!

One of the bunch stated as he raised a stop watch, begin now. (on your mark, get ready… GO!) I was in no hurry and took my time to read every question from beginning to end. These state tests have four answers to the question. Every now and then there may a fifth on that would be "All or None of the above". Two of the answers are so far out there you can eliminate them very quickly. The two that are left are very similar and the difference between them being one word so reading them all was essential. One by one I read the question, then the answers… eliminated two and choose between what was left. It seemed like I was in there for a long time and a couple of people finished early… I thought I was having a hard time. I finally got to question number two hundred and picked my answer. I did not review my paper, I just stood up and walked to the table and turned it in.

As we exited we were allowed to leave because the results would not be in until later that evening. I went home, took a nap and then started to get ready for the party. There might be one thing I just left out… one of the academy directors pulled me to the side before I left SFA and told me I did a great job and to enjoy my night, gave me a wink and went back inside the building. I didn't know until later that my test had already been graded or run through the machine. There were over forty people took that test… all of them were now friends and I was concerned about some of them not passing. The state allowed a person to take the test three times to achieve a passing score and if it isn't passed by then the student must retake the complete academy if they choose to be in law enforcement. Well, this was only round one so maybe everyone did okay… I hoped.

Later that evening my wife and I headed towards the party and when we arrived there were several students and spouses already there. They were talking about the test results and the score they received. I had not heard a word yet and now I began to get concerned. I looked around for the academy director and didn't see him so I questioned another student and he told me they were supposed to call a number after four o'clock and get the scores. I must have left too early to hear that information so I got the number from him and was headed for a pay phone. I never made it to a pay phone as I ran across the director and asked him did he know my score. He started to laugh at me and said… I will never forget. "Boy… you made the highest score so far on that test." I asked if I had outscored my competitor and he told me. "You don't understand, this is a brand new test and you have the highest score of anyone/" What? What did he say?

I knew what it felt like to be on top and satisfied with a job well done. I had felt satisfaction when I walked away from a building we built and it looked good. A custom fireplace or patio or many other structures we built over the years. Listening to customers brag on our work and signing my name to a set of drawings… seeing the completed structure. Seeing my two boys growing up, well you get the drift, I was satisfied. Now I was satisfied that I had made it through the police academy with the scores I had. I really had something to celebrate… everything!

I did enjoy the party that evening and consumed a few adult beverages and then a few more. Sure was glad I had a driver that evening. There was a bit of a downfall though… several of the students, my friends now, didn't pass the test and one of them was very close to me. I felt bad for this man that I admired and hoped he would do better on his next try. He did enjoy the party though and at least he showed a character trait that not many have. I was still excited and on Monday morning I was going to become a police officer. I had my state certification and now only needed to ink the paper and be commissioned (from the city). A quick swearing in before a judge and I would fulfill a major dream. After the party ended... I think I was taken home because I woke up Saturday morning in my own bed with one hell of a headache. But it felt good!

Chapter 8

Hello Monday morning, the moment I had been waiting for… a long time. I arrived at the Police station along with my friend from the academy they had also hired ready for whatever was going to be thrown my way. First things first though and the paperwork started, lots of things to fill out but if that's what it took, okay! Now off to the emergency room for a physical and then back here. At the ER we waited and waited and finally a doctor arrives to help us out. A typical physical with the turn your head a cough and one added little attraction… bend over and spread your butt cheeks. What? I don't really know what he was looking for up my ass, but I guess he didn't find it.

My friend who was a curtain away told me on the way back to the station that when he heard the doctor say that to me, he said to himself… "What the hell are they looking for? Oh crap" (no pun intended). Back to the station for our swearing in as officers to make it all official. As we stood before the judge and repeated the oath, I got a feeling of pure pride and had to control a smile that wanted out. I had achieved a dream and could not wait to notify my parents about it.

We continued to be inducted so to speak… we were told to pick out some uniforms from a pile of old ones and ordered any gear we may need. The uniform thing wasn't as bad as you may think because they measured us for new ones but it would take a while for them to arrive so the old ones were temporary. Holsters, handcuffs, belts and anything else we needed were issued or ordered. I elected to use my 1911 but the department issued me a .357 revolver anyway. Only a handful of officers were still carrying revolvers then, but everyone had one. Then reality sort of hit… they measured us for a ballistic vest. This was a little eerie if you thought about it too long but also it was something that could save your life. We were given our shifts and we both were placed on evening shift.

There were three shifts, 6:00 am to 2:00 pm, 2:00 pm to 10:00 pm and 10:00 pm to 6:00 am. We would spend time on all three, in dispatch and a week with the detectives during our FTO (Field Training Officer) training period. Last but not least we were assigned our FTO's and were allowed to get to know them a bit. Now report tomorrow for your shift, and be on time… ROOKIE!

My career as a peace officer was about to begin. I admit when I looked in the mirror prior to leaving the house, I liked what I saw, me in a police uniform. I arrived at the station at least thirty minutes early. This was a habit I learned from my dad… always be early and never be late. I still practice this today; I'm always early to everything. I waited for the second shift to arrive and let them all be seated before I sat down. I certainly didn't want to piss anyone off on the first day. As it turned out, my friend and I were on this shift only for the first week as an orientation and we would be changing shifts the following Monday. He was going to third shift and I to second.

Now time for briefing… the shift lieutenant began by introducing my friend and I then moved on to going over the calls that the first shift had. He then discussed where extra patrol was needed and anything special that was to be accomplished that day. Advised us of traffic problems and now time to assign districts. My first training officer was a designated Traffic Unit so I would be working traffic, which by the way is everywhere in the city. Then the districts were assigned… north, south, east and west and lastly an ALL officer to back up or cover or whatever was needed that evening. Sometimes there would be two traffic units and they would split the city in half for coverage.

The first few hours my FTO and I spent driving around town getting me familiar with certain areas. He did all the driving and talking and I did all the listening. We figured out who we knew and who we were related to and so on. We would stop and go over paperwork that would be required later on and again… the war stories. We went back to the station and continued to go over procedures and reports and how the department expected them to look like. We were sitting at the briefing table going over a traffic accident report when my first call came over the radio.

"207" My FTO replied "207 go ahead" then dispatch "aggravated assault (then the address) actor may be on scene, would you back 210". My FTO lock at me and said "we're up, let's roll" We got in the car; he was driving and on with the lights, then on went the siren… damn, one Adam 12. Through town we went, people moving out to the way and you could hear the other officers responding over the radio and through the air. Rolled up to a house and about three other police cars did as well… everybody out in a hurry. We made entry in this house and the first thing he showed me was a huge butcher knife stuck in a wall and blood on the floor. Son of a bitch… first call, really?

We were back up to the officer called there so after the arrest was made and injured party had been loaded in an ambulance we were 10-8 and headed for the emergency room. I was taking all this in, watching and listening to everything going on. My FTO asked if I had seen the knife in the wall before he pointed it out. No I hadn't and that was a good lesson for me that evening, always be aware of your surroundings. A few minutes went by and, "207, major 10-50." We were now on our way to an accident with probable injuries. Lights flashing and siren blaring again we arrived to the accident, a car and motorcycle.

Of all the things for me to be at... a motorcycle accident... Right? I watched as my FTO checked on the condition of the drivers first thing. They were all treatable and would most likely survive. He advised dispatch to go ahead and get the ambulance on the way, code two. That simply meant have them hurry but no need for siren. He had me talk with the motorcycle rider while he spoke to the vehicle driver. Yes sir, you read that right, I actually got to help. I watched as he made a rough sketch of the scene and called in a wrecker to take the motorcycle to a shop. The car was drivable. Then back in the car and back to the hospital to check on injuries to the rider. The whole thing took maybe thirty minutes and another thirty to fill out the accident report. I helped him all the way and when he got to the diagram, I told him I was a draftsman so he allowed me to draw the scene... although he checked it carefully before filing it.

Amazing how that came together so well and then... "207, Major 10-50 (address) and we were back in the car with flashing lights and siren headed for another accident. Two vehicles, one traffic light and somebody wasn't paying attention. No injuries so another process of gathering information for an accident report. I was not supposed to be able to help during orientation, but this FTO let me help where I could. About the time we finished up that report... you guessed it,

"207, 208 is responding to a disturbance, can you back him" My FTO replied "10-4, in route" This went on for a while and it finally was almost 10:00pm and my first day as a police officer was coming to an end. We returned to the station and he showed me how to put everything up for the shift, told me I did a good job and that he would see me the next day. We shook hands and as I was walking towards my car I met up with my classmate and he asked if my evening had been eventful… his was sort of boring. That night after I got home I couldn't stop talking about my day and fortunately for me my wife listened and encouraged me.

The next day was almost a carbon copy of the first. I was allowed to help and we did around six or seven accidents with reports. Again we were in and out of the emergency room and running up and down the roads. Although the day was a busy one and sometimes pressed for time, it was also exciting and fun at the same time. Wednesday and Thursday were the weekend, off for those two days and back to Friday, I mean Monday, I mean… I don't know, it was a work day. Loads of accidents to work and some had very serious injuries. I didn't know going into this how I would react to seeing people injured or dead but so far so good. I was doing well with the sights and sounds of the job and my FTO told me every night that I would make a good officer. I had been told that after my orientation week I would remain with this FTO for three weeks, go to third shift for three weeks and then to first shift for three weeks. After a week in CID (Criminal investigation Division) then I would go through a GHOST week where I would return to my first FTO and be responsible for doing everything during a shift while he only observed. Your work load increased as you made your way through the program form 0% in orientation to 100% in your ghost week. After successfully completing all that you would be assigned a shift and a number.

The next week started out about the same except my FTO was allowing me to do a lot of the work. He told me I was taking to this type of work really fast and pretty much just guided me through situations. He would have never let me bite off more than I could chew and would step in whenever he saw something getting out of hand. We would answer a call or work an accident and then discuss what we did and why we did it. He was still doing most of the driving and told me one day that we were going to work some radar on University Dr. (remember that street?) He drove up and down University and would turn around on a speeding vehicle to pull them over. He taught me how to see an expired inspection sticker while moving and we did a few of those as well. He turned on a vehicle and got them to pull over and as I was looking at the radar speed he told me, "This one is yours."

Holy crap… I had never written a ticket before. I had never told someone they were speeding. I asked if he was sure and he told me sooner or later you're going to have to do this so why not now. He was right but I was nervous. I got out of the passenger side door and slowly walked up to the driver's side of the vehicle. I followed every safety precaution that was taught to us at the academy and as I approached the window a squeaky little voice said, "Did I do something wrong officer?" Man this little lady could have been my mother, I looked at my FTO and he looked at me and I asked for her driver's license. She handed it to me and I questioned if something was wrong and all the things you ask when stopping someone and she told me she just wasn't paying attention. I wrote out the ticket and thanked her for her cooperation… (70 in a 50mph zone). When I got back in the car my FTO told me I had the hard part over because the first ticket was always the hardest one to write. He also complimented me for thanking her for her cooperating and for not telling her to have a nice day. Nothing will piss you off worse than a cop telling you to have a nice day after he just wrote you a ticket... your day had just been messed up.

On to the next one and he was right, I wasn't as intimidated on the following citations and was a little more confident in myself as each day passed. The training continued and my FTO was damn good at showing me the ropes of this business. He allowed me to take on more and more of the responsibility way ahead of schedule. I begin to work complete traffic accidents and there were some serious ones too... He would guide me through it and watch every move I made. As soon as we finished up again, we would find a place to park and discuss what had happened and how to improve on what was done. Make no mistake though... if I became too relaxed, he would let me know. He would remind me just how dangerous our job was and how it could turn to shit in a hurry.

One particular accident involving a passenger car and an eighteen wheeler kept us busy for hours one afternoon. There was a chemical spill and the fire department was called in to wash down the pavement... my first time to witness this. There were no major injuries, thankfully, but I did learn quite a bit about what had to be taken care of at certain accident scenes. One after the other, I continued to work accidents and every now and then got the chance to take a regular call. This particular training period was three weeks long and there were some exciting and tense moments that happened every night. I remember a high speed chase we got in one night right before shift change... and I was driving! As I was working radar one night, about to call it a night, another one of our units started pursuing a vehicle only a few blocks from where we were. My FTO told me to go with him and back him up and I advised the dispatcher of what we were doing. We made our way over to the street he was on just about the time the suspect vehicle came past us headed out of the city. The other city unit was maybe seventy five feet back and as Roscoe P. Coltrane says… "In hot pursuit." We fell in behind them and out into the county we went. I was a little leery about driving fast because I didn't want to tear up a police car being a Rookie and all and besides that, these were Chevy Caprices and didn't handle very well. I started losing some ground on them and my FTO told me to catch them… OK, it's on now! I put my foot in to that Chevy and within a minute we were right behind them. All of a sudden, the car we were chasing started to spin out and went in a parking lot made of white gravel. There was dust everywhere and the driver just kept going in circles until we could no longer see anything except headlights.

We finally had him sort of pinned up against a building and had blocked his ways out because a third police car had arrived by now… and it was the shift sergeant. He was not too happy about the fact that two of his patrol units were outside the city, that and the fact he didn't know why his patrol cars were chasing in the first place. The driver of the fleeing vehicle was removed from the driver's side and he was laughing… loud. I had never seen anything like this before but the other officers seem to treat it like it was an everyday event. The driver threw a lot of curse words out there and the other officers just replied… "Yeah, yeah, yeah" as they handcuffed him and placed him in the back of a patrol car. To this day, I don't know why he ran. The officer that initiated the pursuit said he just took off when he passed by him. Our theory is he had something illegal and threw it out during the chase but… he might have been just bat shit crazy, guess I'll never know. We ended that night on a peaceful note with nobody hurt and by the way… that's the way I wished all nights would end but it isn't.

The rest of the evening shift training pretty well went without any major snafus as I continued to work nearly all of the responsibilities. Accidents dominated the calls and traffic control was in down time. Lots of tickets were written, lots of beer poured in a pasture... wait a minute, I haven't told that story yet. One Friday night around dark my FTO and I made plans with the other traffic officer to work a place called Northview Plaza. Now the plaza is where the cinemas are and a weekend hangout for the teenagers. Behind the plaza was a large pasture that belonged to a local business man. The kids would get their beer go to Northview Plaza. This was mostly local High School aged kids because SFA University had more private parties. This sort brought back memories of the "woodsies" I attended during my years in High School. Anyway, we would sit on the backside in the dark and as they arrived would only have to watch for a short time before one would get a beer from their trunk or back of their truck. (There are lots of trucks in Nacogdoches) Once they started, we would intervene before the drinking started. We would have them pour out the beer in the pasture... and not the floorboard like what happened to me. Then have them call parents (no cell phones then only pay phones) to let them know what they were up to. To this day I believe the livestock in that pasture smiled a lot. It worked well and most of the parents took it well... and appreciated them not going to Juvenile Probation. I stated most parents... right? There were a few that complained about the wastefulness of this act and threatened with their attorneys. Anyway, these days you can't do stuff like that because someone always complains.

Now as I was winding up my evening shift of training, I knew I was headed the nightshift (10:00 pm – 6:00 am) and guess what? Yes, I was assigned to another traffic officer for training. This was to be an eye opening experience in more ways than one. Right off, I was given the FTO my last one warned me about… told me he was an asshole. I wasn't all that pleased with the selection but it really didn't matter because I would only be with him for three weeks. Hell, I could do anything for three weeks. The very first night he told me that he didn't care if I was friends with the chief and he didn't care how highly I was being talked about… he would have me in remedial training if I screwed up. So, from the start… I liked him too! I had never done a DWI stop or performed any sobriety tests on the streets and that would be his first question. So he finds the first drunk driver he can and hands it over to me… no explanation, no instructions, just a shit eating grin. It didn't take long for me to realize my first FTO was right about him, but I was going to succeed despite him. At the end of the shift we made our way to the station for a critique and though I was receiving three and four's for my evaluations he told me he didn't give a five and very few four's to anybody so I should not expect them no matter what. Well, he was right… I went from pretty good to pretty not so good in one day! This guy was a total jerk and one of those types that thought he was the best thing that ever happened to law enforcement.

The officers on the midnight shift are a different breed all together… not a bad thing. Most of them like midnights and do not want off. Midnights offer a different style of policing as well as a different crowd to deal with. There were many alcohol and drug calls… a DWI would be every night at least once. Lots of fights between drunks, college students, family members, with each other and the officers on the scene occurred. This was a real busy time of day right up until around 2:00am. Because that's when the town just went dead. It's like everything sort of stopped. This was no guarantee, but it happened most nights and the ones that didn't would shut down by 3:00am. The officers would park and catch up on paperwork or do extra patrol requests, anything to stay awake. There was a lot of coffee consumed at the station as well during these last few hours of the shift. One specific time I remember well is my FTO and I met up with a female officer one night in a secluded parking lot. He drove nearly all the time because he didn't like the way anyone drove but himself so I was the passenger... always. It was pitch black where we were and there was no traffic on the radio so he turned on the music radio and he got out of the car right into the other car. Hmmm... wonder what they were doing in there? Well whatever it was took around forty five minutes or so and when he returned to the patrol car he advised me that I didn't have to tell everything I knew. Oh hell no... I was pretty tired of the way he was treating me anyway so I replied that he was right, I didn't have to tell everything I knew... and he didn't have to keep underscoring me on my evaluations, deal? Deal!

I finished out my midnight shift training actually on a good note. I learned how to complete the duties of the officers on that shift as well as respect exactly how different their work was. My FTO and I did become friends, well sort of, we got along with each other but you know... there were no friendly afternoon barbeques between the families. All and all it was three weeks that I am glad I had behind me and not to look forward to. Up next for me was going to be a tour on the day shift, the one where an officer gets to really interact with the public. I learned that my FTO was going to be... wait for it... you guessed right, a traffic unit. Could there be a conspiracy here? Three shifts, three traffic units... I was beginning to think I was being trained to be a traffic officer, do they do that?

The few things that did bother me about the midnight shift were really simple things like... you couldn't see the way you should! I was always uncomfortable while working in the dark and probably over cautious but... better safe than sorry, Right? Walking up on a vehicle when it was dark was an eerie feeling and I still don't like it today. The attitudes of people totally change after the sun sets while the use of alcohol and drugs increases. An officer never knows what he or she is walking up on until they get right on top of it... pucker factor up! I do know that I would much rather deal with someone high on weed than drunk on alcohol. I am not trying to tell this is the gospel, but in my dealings with people on weed, they were generally happy and didn't want to fight so much. You could tell them they were going to jail and they (most of them) would agree with you. People drunk on alcohol seemed to want to fight and argue a lot more and sometimes physical force had to be used. And those who were on stronger drugs... it could go either way because some types would cause them to just go limp and others would give them super human strength. I will tell you this... I have a great respect for officers that work midnights and they are very special professionals doing a very special job.

Nobody had warned me that dayshift traffic units worked so many accidents... common sense should have told me but it didn't. Accident after accident all day long and during the few moments in between, we worked radar somewhere. The good was that we were off on Thursday and Friday so it did seem like somewhat of a weekend. My FTO was a seasoned veteran who took a lot of pride in his position. He loved working traffic and didn't want to do anything else. We became friends almost immediately and worked well together for years afterwards. Although there was no such thing as a ticket quota, (many people think there is) my FTO always wanted to be the top writer of the department. At the end of every shift the dispatcher would call your number and ask for citations. It would be like "207, citations" " 207, three moving, three radar, one warning"

My FTO had numbers like "twenty three moving, twenty radar" and he was good at it. I must have tripled my ticket writing during those weeks with him except on Sunday mornings. On Sunday mornings the drivers got a little break because my FTO went to every car dealership in town and looked at new cars. I do not know how long he had been doing this routine but it seemed to work for him and maybe was his few minutes of down time for the week. Seems every day when we were ready to call in our totals, I would get the evil eye from my FTO, his theory was "We are a traffic unit, we are supposed to enforce traffic laws and that means writing tickets and working wrecks" Period!

These were fun weeks even though they were busy. Run, Run, Run and it made the day go by quick. Biggest problem here was complaints from the public... yeah they had them before nowadays. You know I was never a big writer about certain things, blinker for changing lanes for example. As long as it was safe, what the hell? But if I didn't use a blinker, someone called the station and complained. We as officers are complained on for everything in the traffic code even if they are not enforced. Everyone who has smoked has at one time flipped a cigarette out of the window, but you better not as an officer. Even when you were allowed to smoke, better not let the public see because they would complain. I had never in my life seen anything like it... complain about everything. Everything from the way the hair was worn to the type of shoes an officer had on. Complaints about driving, language, dress, habits, attitude, knowledge... from A to Z if it could be complained about, it was. Complaints about over reacting, too much force, and even not enough force were a common thing. Please don't misunderstand, there were officers that needed complained on but they were few and far between. Anyway by this time I was doing all the work and so far... really adapting to police work. I learned quite a bit from this FTO and still keep in touch with him today. My next stop would be a week in CID (Criminal Investigations Division) to work with the detectives as well as the crime scene processor.

I had been looking forward to this week because to me this was what it was all about. This is where I wanted to be eventually and I knew every detective at the department and held them in high regards. I was assigned an FTO of course and this week I was to wear a coat and tie. Again I was being trained in another different way of enforcing the law... confused yet? The week in CID was very different because you would take over where the patrol officer left off. The detectives would take a report on a class B or above crime and start working it up. You may do a warrant request and it would be simple or a full blown investigation that could take some time. I learned to take a statement from a victim as well as a defendant. Reading rights was to become second nature to me later on but for now it was new. Going into homes and businesses to interview and question people was exciting and fun. However... it was nothing like on TV or in the movies and I mean nothing. There was no glamour, just good folks doing an honest job trying to make a difference. I was always told that cops only arrested the bad guys but it's not true, they also help the victims. For every person that claims that the cops "did this to me" there is another that claims the cops "did this for me" I was lucky during this period because I was able to work on a sexual assault (rape) case. I call this lucky due to the fact that in the future I would work many of these type cases with much success.

I was able to learn how to request misdemeanor and felony warrants, search warrants and how to properly fill out all types of documents needed for an investigation. I found myself really wanting to be in this level of police work and would set my goals to do this as fast as possible due to my late start into this career. I was living my dream of being in police work and then GHOST WEEK arrived. This was my last week in training and everything was to be done by me without help except in time one would need back up anyway. The FTO which was my first week and evening FTO was my ghost rider. I was to make all decisions and complete all the proper paperwork and score well on my evaluation to become an officer on my own. To this point I had a very successful training period and I wasn't about to let this week intimidate me… I was confident and ready when I showed up again on evening shift. And yes, I was a traffic unit… what else? One week ahead of being on my own and as I sat around the conference table listening to the briefing a familiar sound came over the speaker… "Major 10-50, North at Starr" So it began… I had a major accident to work and briefing wasn't even over. Out the door and in the car we went along with another officer for traffic control.

North Street and Starr Avenue is a main intersection located right at the SFA campus and normally extremely busy. At 6:00am, however, it's a manageable traffic control. I arrived at the scene and placed my vehicle blocking the area of the accident. An ambulance had arrived and the EMT's were placing one of the drivers on a stretcher. I started to gather my information and checked with the EMT personnel regarding the condition of the drivers. One driver was okay and the other had non-life threatening injuries. Now I knew I had plenty of time to get everything right and I started collecting what I needed for the report. Vehicle information, insurance information, witness statements and drivers information. I wrote all this down on an accident form so I would remember what all I needed but it was a rough copy. After I finished up I released the scene to the wrecker drivers who begin to clear the scene and off to the hospital

I went. My FTO had not said a word, but did have a big smile on his face and I know he knew he had done a good job when training me. At the hospital, I spoke to the driver and he explained he never saw the other vehicle and also told me of some other details I needed… then I determined that he was at fault and issued a citation. After all that, I went 10-8 (back in service) and requested permission to return to the station to complete my report. The dispatcher politely told me that she had a minor 10-50 holding and for me to take it. Wow, I thought… is the day going to be like this… survey says, YES!

I was sent to eight accidents that first day and had a pile of reports to complete. In those days, you could have a report pending for twenty four hours with approval from the department so I had to do this for several of them. After the shift though, I stayed at the station and completed every one of those reports so by briefing the next morning I was ready to go with a clean slate. (Ha Ha Ha, I'll show them) I am glad I did stay and finish because the following morning started out very much in the same manner. Accident after accident, then I was sent to back up on a couple of disturbance calls and this continued most of the shift. Towards the end, however, there was about a two hour period of quiet and although it was very uncommon, I took advantage of it along with my lunch to complete all the reports. Every single one of those were completed and turned in… I felt good. I actually got to go home that day on time. Home at that time was a rented house we had found through a friend. It was small but comfortable and the cost to live there was low. I had just spent a couple of months in the academy with no pay and now I was in this FTO program with start out pay so things were a little on the thin side. I was fortunate that my wife had a good job and her income kept everything going during this period. We had sold all the toys we had to prepare for this so we did okay. Going home on time was a luxury and sitting in a recliner watching television was appreciated. A good night sleep and I was ready for my Wednesday.

I got to work around 1:30 pm on Wednesday and hung out around the squad room while having a little coffee. One of the dispatchers told me that the day had been slow and not many calls other than assistance needed had come in. Could it be true? Would I get a day like that? Was there such a thing as a slow day? The answer was… yes. I started out driving around and no calls… I sort of didn't know what to do until a light came on! Work some radar… and so I set up at my favorite spots and started monitoring vehicle speeds. After a few tickets, I worked some moving radar and inspection sticker checks and again wrote a few tickets. This went on most of the day and I encountered so many different types of people with their different types of responses and excuses it was actually amusing at times. Some of the reasons for traffic violations were funny and some were not, but it sure made the day go by fast. I returned to the station at around 9:45pm and just as I pulled up to gather my equipment … "207, major 10-50, South at Seale… code three" Really? Crap, a code three, I had to hurry because that meant to run with lights and siren due the possibility of a bad injury or fatality. Flip, flip went the switches and lights and siren were on and we were hauling ass to the accident scene. Two other patrol units rolled with us for traffic assistance and kept oncoming cars off of us. As I pulled up to the accident scene I could see three vehicles involved and a person laying in the road way. The ambulance had not arrived and I immediately responded to the person in the road… he was breathing but in bad shape. I called the dispatcher and requested the ambulance to hurry and in a few minutes they arrived. My FTO didn't just watch on this one… it was bad and he helped out tremendously. Between My FTO and the two officers that assisted me… well let's just say they made it possible for me to do my job that night. Without all of them, I would have been in trouble.

The accident scene was sort of spread out and the other drivers were being removed from their vehicles. EMT personnel was attending to all the injured people as there were passengers in every vehicle… thank goodness all were alive. A second ambulance was called in for transport of the injured and wreckers were called in to remove the vehicles and in the middle of it all was… Me, rookie cop. It took an hour to clear the scene and an additional hour at the hospital checking on all the injuries and interviewing the drivers. It was after midnight and I wasn't about to request a pending status on this one, this was my chance to make a statement about myself. I hung out at the station until I had completed the entire report and turned it in. It was somewhere around 2:30 am so I was able to go home and rest before the next night. I remember when I finally arrived home that night, my wife was mad as hell because I forgot to call and she didn't know where I was. That was my fault, I was so wrapped up in to finishing what I had to do that I totally forgot about everything else… the important things. This would haunt me in the future and I should have paid more attention. So… bring on my Thursday 'cause I ain't skeered.

I remember Thursday being a rainy day and I was a little tired from the night before so that pretty much set the scene for my day. Rainy days meant accidents and on my way to work I was thinking… more accidents today, there has to be more than accidents, I need something else besides an accident. Well… not going to happen, so guess what I got called to right after briefing? Yep, an accident. If you missed that question then you failed the test. This was my Thursday and actually Friday because yesterday was my Wednesday but actually Thursday. My first day was my Monday but really Tuesday and tomorrow would be my Friday that happens on a Saturday Got It? Back to my Thursday and it started with a major accident on the loop… a pretty serious injury but they did survive. I was called to a couple of minor accidents mostly just small fender benders and mad drivers. I was able to back up a couple of patrol calls before the night just sort of calmed down. I was able to go on a prowler call before the end of the shift and after a half hour of looking and searching… I found the guy. Way to go Rookie! He was trying to hide by a dumpster but was way too noisy so I heard him. Turned out it was a peeping Tom trying to get an eyeful of the girls living in the house. So I did get credit for the arrest and that ended the night and I was excited because I had one more night until I was a full working Police Officer… I was proud and happy.

My Friday which was actually a Saturday… started out real easy, SFA had a football game in town and a lot of parents were around. Regular public school was out for the weekend so not much going on there either so for a few hours it was peaceful. I spent a little time to work some traffic, not radar, but watching stop signs and traffic lights. I wrote a few tickets but also gave a few breaks to people. Backed up a family disturbance call for one of the patrol units and then it was time for lunch. My FTO and I went to a restaurant (very seldom did we have this luxury) and after the meal, I paid the tab and thanked him for his patience and guidance. This was one of the few times we were able to complete a meal without getting a call. The Patrol units were able to do that because they would just call in another patrol unit or have a traffic unit take it. The traffic unit was expected to respond to all accidents except when on one already. This is not a gripe because it worked well and kept the shift running smooth. We left the restaurant and got back on the streets and about thirty minutes went by and… you got it. "207, major 10-50 Starr at University" well here we go again. The SFA game had let out and someone wasn't paying attention to all the traffic around them. I rolled up on the scene and what did I see? Two cars, one pick -up truck and a motorcycle stuck in a tree.

Oh yes, you read that right… in a tree. I called for other units to control traffic because this accident was spread all over University drive. First there were two cars that had hit head on… then a pick-up truck that had hit a motorcycle and knocked it off the road and into a tree. There was a helmet in the middle of the road and bits and pieces of vehicles everywhere… who wanted to be a police officer? The only thing to do was start on one end and work through something like that and so I did. First things first… are there any injuries? The motorcycle rider was sore but up and walking around and now how about the others? I went ahead and called for an ambulance just because that rider looked like he was in pain and being a motorcyclist, I was concerned about his wellbeing. The truck driver was okay, however, he was mad because he never saw the motorcycle. Now how about them two cars… well both drivers seemed okay but did want to have an EMT look at them, now what the hell happened here? After several interviews and a few witnesses coming forward it went something like this; the pick-up truck was traveling east on Starr at the intersection of University and Starr, a motorcycle was traveling west on Starr both facing green signal lights. The driver of the truck turned left into the path of the motorcycle which caused the motorcycle to hit the truck on its right side. The operator of the motorcycle fell off and the motorcycle veered into a tree located on the northwest corner of the intersection. And now the interesting part… after the light changed a vehicle traveling north on University attempted to avoid the collision by veering to the left and went between the truck and motorcycle striking another vehicle traveling south on University… Got That? What a mess it was, but fortunately nobody was hurt seriously. I spent the rest of my shift that night working on that report. It was like working two accidents, hell it was two accidents. On accident reports the state allows only a small area for the diagram, I had to use a whole piece of paper for mine. The report was finished and the shift was over and… my FTO congratulated me on my successful completion of my training period. I was relieved, happy, proud and yet sad too… I enjoyed these FTO's I had and remained friends with them.

My original FTO passed away several years later, my midnight FTO moved off to the Dallas area and my dayshift FTO, he continued to work for the city and SFA until he retired. He still lives in the area. I was a full time Nacogdoches Police Officer now and was assigned to the day shift as a patrol unit, my number… 210. I got Thursday and Friday as off days and was to report Tuesday morning at 6:00am for duty to my shift lieutenant. The day I had waited for what seemed like forever was upon me and I was ready for it. I spent the next two days mentally preparing for this new job. I cleaned up all my gear and had all my uniforms cleaned and pressed as well as polishing my boots. My family had a celebration dinner for me at a local favorite Mexican food place and best of all… I called my dad and told him I had made it through. I knew he would be happy, but I also knew he wanted me to be working with him. If you haven't figured out by now my dad was and is today my hero. I respect and admire what he was and what he stood for… I loved him with all my heart.

Chapter 9

If I may, let explain about some of the things he did. My dad was like many others in a few ways because he worked and provided for the family. He made sure we always had a comfortable home and nice vehicles. There were a lot of ways he was no different than any other dad but… there were a bunch of ways that set him apart. First of all, he could never say no to anyone in need of help, family or not. I have seen him give days of his time to help out a family member or friend with any request they might have. Whether it be building a neighbors fence or loaning money to someone in need, he just could not say no. He stood right for those who couldn't and by that I mean that he would always take up for a person needing that type of help. Seems every neighborhood we ever lived in, he was the one everybody came to for help. I do not remember any occasion that he let any family member down for any reason. He gave and gave until he had nothing left and then he gave more.

I remember when I first wanted to move out… he was against it but respected that I had to do it and helped me out. This happened several times if you recall. He did the same for my brothers and my middle brother was a handful. He loved kids, all kids. He would do whatever to insure a smile on a kids face. Basically, if you called on him, he was there for the long haul. He loved surprising us with gifts and did so as often as was possible back in the day. He was a very strong person physically as well as mentally.

He was fun to be around too… he took us shopping for a new push lawn mower one day and a comedy show took place. He started out at Sears and looked at mostly basic models then before he would make a decision he wanted to go look at Montgomery Ward (look it up) We arrived at Montgomery Ward and a salesperson approached while he was looking at a simple basis mower. My dad asked how much was the mower and the man replied with an amount and told my dad, "That's a good mower but this is a lot better," pointing to a more expensive model. The salesman gave all the specifics and was really going with a sale pitch. After he finished he asked my dad what he thought now. My dad replied, "That's great but how much is this one?" pointing to the basic model. Here he went again… "Sir, you don't want that one, look at this one," and again my dad thanked him for the information and again he asked how much for the basic model. As the salesman started to tell him that he didn't want that one, my dad turned toward him and said to him, " You're right, I don't want that one or any other mower you have in this store. I'll go somewhere that will sell me the one I want." We went back to Sears and he bought a mower.

He seemed to approach a lot of things like this. The time he bought me my Duster before moving to Nacogdoches was again an experience… we looked at the car and he told the salesman that it was too much for him. I was already in love with it so I thought… "Oh no, I'm not getting this one." He and the salesman went back and forth and finally my dad made him a really low offer on the car. I knew that was it, he would never agree and I wasn't getting that car. The salesman did say he couldn't take that low of an amount and so my dad wrote his name and number on a piece of paper and they shook hands… we went home.

Damn, I wasn't going to get a car that day. It may sound a little selfish but I was only a teenager and was excited and yet let down because my dad had just turned the deal down. If any of you have been there then you know the feeling. I moped around the house for a few hours and wondered if we would go looking for another car. I mentioned to my dad that it was afternoon and we should go to another dealership. He explained that he was waiting on the salesman to call before he looked elsewhere. I was like; really, he told you no... let's move on but he told me he knew I wanted that car and to be patient. Well crap... no car, no time and... ring, ring, ring! "Hello, okay then we will be right down. " It was the salesman and he agreed to my dad's offer. We drove to the dealership and bought the car. Patience... what a concept!

I told you of his physical strength... there wasn't much he grabbed onto that didn't move. He was built like Popeye (look it up) with big chest and huge forearms. He was very powerful and looked it. I remember on a family gathering and we were at my uncle's house in Lufkin, Texas which is only about twenty miles south of Nacogdoches. Anyway, my uncle owned the VW dealership in Lufkin at the time (remember this for later on). My cousin had a flat tire on his car and yes it was a VW Beetle. We could not find a jack anywhere and eventually went to ask for one. Dad came out to the vehicle and looked around for a jack and finally said ya'll get ready to get that tire changed... with that he opened the door and placed his shoulder inside the top frame. Then at our surprise he stood up straight and both drivers side tires came off the ground. Damn! As he stood there, we were in awe and he finally said, "Well, hurry up, I can't stand here all day." We changed the tire. After we finished, my uncle shows up with a jack... we all got a laugh out of that.

The one thing he did that brought tears to my eyes was at Christmas time. I don't know how many times he did this but my mom tells me more than once… I only witnessed it one time. Christmas was my dad's favorite time of the year as it is with many. He loved to give and make people happy. We had one particular employee for the masonry company who had a new wife and family. Financially, they were not very well off (don't know the reason, but it did not matter) It was feared that the kids would not have a good Christmas and this made my dad feel a little sad that year. He gave that employee enough money to make a really good Christmas for those kids and there was no pay back. I still run across one of those kids nowadays although she is grown with her own kids and she remembers that year and along with her mother remind me of what a great person my dad was.

He also was at the local mall with my mother shopping and noticed a Christmas (and by the way, I am going to continue to use the word Christmas and I am NOT going to change) tree that had pieces of paper hung on it instead of ornaments. There were names of children that did not have a way to get a Christmas gift. There were foster kids, underprivileged children and all types of kids that were not going to have Christmas. My parents took a couple of those names off the tree to buy gifts and left. Many people do this every year and it is a wonderful act. Giving a child a Christmas that may not have one is second to none in good deeds. The following day was Christmas Eve and my Mom was going to the mall to pick up a few small things for our family get together. Dad had her gather all the names left on the tree so gifts could be bought before the deadline… he said no kid should go without Christmas.

I tell you all this to make a point... I called my dad to tell him what I did and he told me he was so proud of the decision I made and admired me for making it. He told me he was proud of my accomplishments but he knew I could do it all along. My dad that I admired so much... admired me too. It took a while for all that to soak in.

Chapter 10

Bright and early, my first day on the job as a police officer and I was glad to be there. I had looked into the mirror at home long enough, I was there and ready to go. As the other officers filed in the room, most of them with a cup of coffee in hand, I refilled my cup and walked in with the rest of them. The shift Lieutenant started talking and introduced me as the newest member of the shift. We all knew each other anyway, but it was sort of cool being called a member of the shift. The Lt. started talking about what had happened over night and where he wanted to concentrate on traffic control and… well anything that had to do with the way he wanted this shift to go. This Lt. was an older officer and had been with the department for many years. He was funny and yet serious at the same time and relied heavily on his Sergeant and Corporal to help him run this shift. He had a habit of calling everyone "Young'un" and that started with me on this first day. He started to assign districts to the officers and then the traffic unit, which was my FTO… where do I go? Huh? Huh? He looked at me and said "Young'un, you will be an All unit for a few days." What this meant was I would be able to go anywhere in town and would mostly be a backup unit. I was on my own but I think this Lt. was going to introduce me to the work a little at a time.

The officers on this shift were a unique bunch and these officers were in the public eye more than the other shifts. Most of them were seasoned and knew what they were doing. The Sergeant was a great person with a likable personality. He was easy to friend and easy to work for. He expected you to do your job and talk with him every now and then. He loved to talk about hunting and fishing, well just about everything I enjoyed talking about. It didn't take long to become close. Then there was the Corporal... what a character (not in a bad way) he was. I had heard stories of him for years and now was on shift with him. Gripy, grumpy and hard to get along with... you couldn't help but like this guy. I know this sounds crazy, but you would have had to know him to understand.

Then there was the traffic officer, My FTO and also a seasoned officer. I loved this guy. He had thinning hair and tried to cover it up but it didn't work. He would be my backup on many calls in the future and I was comfortable with him behind me. I had no doubt he would protect me. There was a second traffic officer and he was also a good person, I just had never worked with him much. He and I are still good friends today as well. There was an officer that was towards the end of his career, good as gold and always smiling, a female officer who was a little hard to get to know but was very smart and before I would be through with this shift would teach me a lot and help me be promoted. A business man turned police officer that was a nice guy but full of himself... he liked to flaunt his expensive belongings. There were others that floated in and out however this was primarily a senior officer shift.

So... I was an All unit for the first few days and looking back I am glad that happened. I was able to do several backup calls, mostly disturbances or civil standbys but I was learning how to deal with people more and more. Every call is different and every person you encounter has a different personality. You may be dealing with an individual having the worst day of their life and they truly believe that… wound up and it's up to you to bring them down. You may have to arrest someone which brings me to the end of my first day. A family disturbance call, possibly one of the most dangerous calls for an officer and I was lead officer. Arrived at a house and a man was in the front yard throwing furniture and household things all over the place. A woman was in the house with the doors locked and screaming at him to go away… to which he was using that F-bomb pretty freely when we arrived. I had a backup already there so I started trying to communicate with the guy, trying to get him to calm down and tell me what was wrong. He kept telling me to get away; it was none of my business and slinging the F-bomb over and over. There were three officers on the scene and while two of us were dealing with him the third officer made entry and now was with the woman. The other officer and I got an opening between the throwing and the cursing and tackled the man. Once we had him on the ground, he fought us for just a second and once cuffed he started crying and telling us about what she had done to him. I took the report from the woman and the other officer transported him to jail where I met them and processed him in.

The rest of the day went fairly well right up until another disturbance call. Three brothers in a house and two parents outside was what awaited our arrival. Another unit arrived and I stepped in the door while my back up checked on the folks in the yard. The three boys jumped on me almost immediately and the parents got on my partner. So, while I was getting my ass kicked inside my partner had his hands full outside. I sure was happy when other officers arrived and "saved them boys from me" Yeah, right! Five to jail, lots of paperwork and then…10-42!

I would keep this schedule for about two months and during that period I answered many different type of calls. Shoplifters at local businesses were pretty much a daily happening. One store particularly, yes you guessed it… Wal-Mart had more than its share. Seems like every day the police were called to Wal-Mart and it was usually something small and sometimes just didn't make sense. It may not have been every day but it was often and when I saw what the person was stealing, I would just shake my head. Makeup was a popular item… yeah Makeup! Razor blades also seemed to walk out the door quite often. The other items were condoms and pregnancy tests… I guess they sort of went together. It always went the same way or so it seemed, we arrived and walked to the back of the store to a small office where the offender was along with a loss prevention officer and a manager. The offender usually told us that the store people were lying on them and they didn't do anything. Every now and then someone would just tell it like it was and say they stole it and cooperated completely. We would write or sign a receipt so the store could get their merchandise back and handcuff the offender. Out to the patrol car and down to the station. This was before tickets were written for Cass C thefts. An agent from the store came to the station to sign a complaint and off to jail the offender went. There was very little trouble however, there is always that one person that wants to fight about it and there were times we had to take someone to the ground and forcefully remove them from the store… I didn't like those times but they did happen.

There were family disturbances and civil disputes we answered regularly along with unruly customers in stores. We had bank escorts and standbys… every now and then an officer would have to respond to the station to take a complaint of some sort and it could be anything. Of course there were plenty of accidents and traffic control and this was every day, all day! I suppose being in a college town that accidents do happen a little more often. We also had to answer calls to the school district if they had a problem and there were problems that occurred on our campuses. The times it flooded in Nacogdoches, which was every time it rained for a day or two, we responded to help needed calls and actually waded into flooded areas to carry people out or assist them in several different ways. I have had to clean up my leather gear and equip more than once because it got soaked during one of these floods. Boots would stay wet for days afterwards and I always kept an extra pair around the house.

Speaking of around the house, my wife and I had finally saved up enough money and with help from her parents, bought a new house during this period. It was a nice house in a nice neighborhood, but it was not new so we had to have a few things done before we moved in. She wanted the carpets cleaned even though they didn't look bad so I started looking for a cleaning service. The Captain at the police department was just starting up a cleaning and chemical service so we hired his people to do the job. His people turned out to be him and he made the carpet look and smell brand new. You know that he and I are friends today and I'll tell you about that a little later on.

So we got all moved in thanks to the help from my new family… fellow officers helped us get settled. I asked for help and officers started showing up in pick-up trucks and some pulling trailers, I'll tell you it didn't take very long to move everything with all that help. The Blue Brotherhood (and Sisterhood) is for real, right? You bet it is! I loved the family, the new house, and the way I made a living now so what more could I want? I answer that with… time with my wife and kids. Something had to be done about quality time spent with them. The problem was, I had only been with the department for a few months so no vacation time had accumulated. I would have to wait a year for a good vacation, until that happened I needed to spend afternoons and evenings at home. There is one thing that most officers will agree on and that is a second job is a necessity in order to obtain more than the essentials. So what happened? I'll tell you... I started taking on side security jobs. Well so much for spending evenings and weekends with my family. I worked at the local mall and several other local stores until the dollar income was really good. We were able to buy all sorts of things and keep the needs of two growing boys fulfilled. Seems every time I felt good about our financial situation that monster of more time for the family reared his ugly head. I was succeeding as an officer, but failing as a father. More on this to come later.

Back at work, I was called into the Lieutenant's office one morning after briefing and told to sit down. Oh shit... what the hell had I done? This office wasn't quite big enough for one person much less two so we were real close together. Lt. was working on some paperwork and I just sat there trying to think of what I did that would have me in his office. Had I been rude to someone? Had I mistreated someone? I didn't have a clue what I could have done. He kept on with his paperwork and I know he knew I was sweating this out... he would turn his head towards me every now and then and, "Young-un, Young-un , oh lord" and then shake it with an "Umph, umph, umph." After a while he gathered up his paperwork and left the office. Okay... what the hell was going on? I surely must have pissed off the wrong person and for the life of me, couldn't think of anything. I was getting uncomfortable and started moving in the chair. Lt. entered back in the room with two cups of coffee and handed me one... "Black, right?" "Yes sir, thank you," then silence again. After about half a cup he finally asked if I wondered why I was called in the office. When I told him I had been trying to think of a reason, he replied, "OH, there is a reason... a good reason." "What is it?" He turned to me and cleared his throat and rubbed his hand across his mouth... "Hmmm." He was so serious and said. "I have a decision to make and that decision depends on how you answer a question."

By this time, I was about to explode and he rubbed his mouth again and grinned... he owned me! He was grinning and asked. "Are you interested in a Traffic Officer position on this shift?" I'll tell you I must have turned a couple of shades of red, but it only took a second for me to answer him... "Yes Sir!" Wow! my Lt. told me that I had been turning in some of the best accident reports and offense reports he had ever read. Really? Me. the rookie. I hit the streets that morning knowing that the following morning he would announce the news to the rest of the shift.

Chapter 11

The following morning it was announced that I would be a traffic unit and my new number would be 207. I changed epilate color tabs from green to red and was back doing what I did best in training. I don't even recall what happened that first day on traffic, I was on cloud nine most of the day adjusting to the new role. I remember working a few minor accidents and maybe a parking lot fender bender. I also recall writing a few tickets but mostly a regular day… we like regular days oh yes we do. I did change to Friday and Saturday as off days and remember thinking that I would have a weekend day to do things with my family now. The rest of that week went by fast and I continued to work my area of town… for some reason I was nearly always assigned to the north side where the university is located. Wal-Mart, North View Plaza and the cinemas were there too. And last but not least, Medical Center Hospital was in the north traffic district so I had a plateful and plenty to keep me busy every day. I had been very fortunate not to have worked a fatality accident and that would change come the following Monday morning.

That following Monday during briefing, a familiar sound… "207, 208, 204, Major 10-50 code 3 Southeast Stallings at the plywood plant" That was me, a patrol unit and a supervisor being called to an accident… it has to be bad. We all took off from the station in a hurry, the patrol unit out front. I was behind because I had to load my equipment; the sergeant grabbed a traffic camera before he left. I was almost to the scene when I heard 208 check out on the scene. The officer called for traffic control unit as the loop was totally blocked. I topped a hill and there it was… a log hauler loaded with logs and a passenger car, I think. I positioned my vehicle and when I stepped out of my car, I slipped in something. It was diesel fuel from the log hauler tank. I radioed the other units to not allow anyone to smoke in the area and for the fire department to respond and do a wash down. What a mess…there were pieces of vehicle everywhere. The diesel smell was overwhelming and burned the eyes and throat. I saw the driver of the log hauler and was looking to see if the driver of the car was anywhere… someone yelled out "He's still in the car."

Oh crap, the car was crushed down to about three feet tall as the roof was even with the hood and trunk. It was still dark and I shined my flashlight inside the car to see fingers in the door pocket, no hand, just fingers. I could tell that a body was in there and called for Rescue 5 (the Fire Department specialty vehicle for accidents) and the Jaws of Life. The patrol units did a great job of routing the traffic flow around the scene and I started to do my job. As with any accident there were statements from witnesses and talk with the driver of the log hauler. All the accounts of the accident matched up so it was getting clearer as to what had happened. The fire department had not removed the body from the car so I continued to mark reference points and take measurements. After much effort, the crew was able to reach the body and his wallet. Now I had a name and address of the driver. This was a man in his thirties over six foot tall and two hundred pounds. His body was pinned between the steering column and the door post of the car in an area about four inches thick… yeah, four inches.

The EMT teams were there and they helped the Fire Department in removing the body and I continued on with my investigation. I made a rough draft of the scene and added the measurements. Things included in a drawing were traffic signals or control signs, intersections, shoulders, lanes and type of striping along with the position of each vehicle and which direction they came from and on and on. I took pictures off everything I did and by the time I got back to the car they were removing the body from the mangled vehicle including the fingers in the door cup. The EMT's could not say he was deceased so they left with him in the ambulance and I followed them to the hospital, while the Sergeant saw to the cleaning of the scene. That is team work, make no mistake... teamwork.

At the hospital, it was some formal things that had to be taken care of before the body was released to a funeral home. An autopsy was ordered but it was apparent what he died from. The reason was to check for any foreign substance in his blood. I finished up, took a big breath and headed for the station to start my report, my first fatality accident report. After I had finished the written report and filled out the state form all that was left to do was a drawing and I elected to do it at home on my drafting table so I requested a pending status on the complete report and... went back out on the streets. I finished my shift and it probably wasn't the most productive afternoon, but I had that fatality on my mind and so I just don't imagine I gave 100% at the end of the day. I took home my field notes and rough drafts so I could do the drawing after supper.

When I started that sketch, I had no intention of doing a scale drawing but it wound up being one. I had learned not to mark a drawing as scale because of the opposition you could run into at trial. I was told that an attorney would shred me on the stand if I listed it as to scale. So even though I drew it to scale, I didn't advertise it. It took a couple of hours to complete the drawing and finish up the total report to be turned in the next morning. I was proud to have signed my name to that report because I took my time on it and I took it seriously… it was more than just a wreck, it was a person's life. The following morning I turned my complete report in and after briefing and telling the shift about the situation… 10-41 Traffic north, hit the streets. Now I had to move on from this one and be ready for the next one.

But this day would have something for me… nothing bad but I couldn't stop thinking about the accident, the sight of that man and the smell of diesel. I don't remember what happened the rest of that day but it must have passed by quickly because before I knew it, time to go home and little to show of the day. So you see, moving on took a little more than I anticipated but it did happen. You know it's said that Murphy's Law will always get you when you least expect it… it's true. The following week about 8:00am… "207, 209, 204, major 10-50 northwest loop code 3." The address placed it in front of a gas well service business in the southbound lanes and my first though was… another 18 wheeler, damn.

I had to approach the scene from the south meaning I had to pass it then turn around and come back to it and I remember seeing a salt water transporter, a van and an engine in the middle of the loop… yeah a motor. I positioned my vehicle and the patrol units got in place to start diverting traffic. There was gasoline everywhere this time and we were basically standing on a bomb. I truly do not know how there was no explosion with all the gouges in the pavement. One would have thought a spark or two would have ignited the fumes but so far so good. One of the officers called for the fire department for a wash down however when they did arrive a foam was used for extra safety, and then the wash down began. I checked on the passengers in the van and an EMT turned to me from the passenger side and shook his head… I knew what that meant. They were removing the driver and he was alive but not responsive. I told them I would meet them at the hospital and stayed to finish up my scene. Again… statements, measurements, vehicle information and so on. This van had struck the back of a salt water truck so hard it actually knocked the engine out and on the ground.

After concluding my scene investigation I had to get to the hospital, I didn't know if the man would live or not. Once at the ER, it was confirmed that the female passenger had died, but the male driver was going to pull through. Information revealed that this was an elderly couple that traveled all the time. The contents of the van showed that as it was full of camping type equipment suitcases and all sorts of traveling conveniences. A doctor came out of one of the trauma rooms and told me I could talk to the man, but he had not been informed of the death of his wife. The doctor and I went in the room together to advise him of what had happened… it was one of the saddest things I had ever witnessed and my eyes teared up. I never cried but I did have to wipe my eyes a couple of times while talking with him about how the accident took place. Are you ready for this?… trying to read a road map. We had almost completed our conversation when the elderly man asked where the van was. I told him which wrecker had towed it and where it was and he looked panicked. When I questioned him about it, he started crying and told me every dime they had was in a briefcase in the van. He was afraid someone would take it and he would have nothing to get home. I knew the owner of the wrecker very well and drove there when I left the hospital. I retrieved the briefcase and took it back to the man. I found out later there was thirty thousand dollars in that briefcase. Not much return on the life of one's spouse.

Days went by and I was doing the job I was assigned… and very well according to my Lt. The days turned to weeks and there were many accidents and calls that I responded to, there was very little time for boredom. One of the sayings for officers is that the job is 90% boredom and 10% pure adrenaline rush. I don't think that is quite accurate. One rainy morning I was sent on a sick call. A sick call is when an ambulance is dispatched to a location for a pick up and it is an unknown situation. Officers are sent just in case there is problem or possibly a crime scene. All of our patrol units were tied up so I was sent. I arrived at an apartment complex and the ambulance had already parked and the back doors were open. As I went in the residence, I observed two EMT's attending to a young boy. They were rushing around and I asked what was going on. "He's unresponsive… maybe a seizure" "We need your help." I was instructed to help clear a path through the room to get him out and once we reached the door, I was told to help stabilize his head while they maneuvered all the tight corners and steps. We reached the ambulance and got him loaded and I was in the back with an EMT. All the way to the hospital this young man stared into my eyes and the EMT and I were trying to get him to respond… nothing. After arrival at the hospital, as we were unloading this child… his eyes got still and he exhaled hard and then he wasn't breathing. My God, had this child just died while in my arms? I went numb with sadness and in a few minutes the ER doctor confirmed his death. I felt like my heart had just fallen out… he was twelve years old and I had a twelve year old son.

The shift sergeant picked me up and returned me to my vehicle. I was down and he could tell so he told me to go to the station and take a break. I went to the locker room which was a small room containing a toilet, a shower, a sink, and a bench and sat down on the bench. While there I must have had a thousand questions run through my brain. Why? Why? Is being a cop all about dealing with death? I was sinking lower and lower and thoughts of quitting the department started running through my head. I wasn't cut out for this, I wasn't made to deal with these tragedies. The longer I sat there the worse it got and even when my Sergeant came in to check on me, I still was having a very hard time. My eyes were watered, my nose was running... I was hurting. About the time I had made up my mind to resign there was a knock on the door and I muttered to come in.

There stood the Captain. Remember the Captain I mentioned earlier that was starting a cleaning business? This was the man that officers feared and mocked... this was the man that tied black thread across driveways after telling officers to patrol somewhere and if that thread wasn't broken... well that was your ass. This was the last person I needed talking to me at this time. I sat there and was waiting for him to tell me to get up and get back to work. I was prepared for an ass chewing about how this was no way for an officer to act... I was waiting. He took me by total surprise when he asked in a soft voice "May I come in?" What? Really? All I could say was "Yes, Sir." He walked through the door and sat beside me, reached over and patted my knee and told me that we could work this out. We were there for well over an hour while he explained what I was going through. Here all along I thought I was getting in trouble and I was getting a reassuring, confidence building talk from a man with years of experience. I told you earlier that we were friends still today and we are. I have a great respect for this man. Between him, my shift Lt. and my Chief of Police I was able to work everything out and get through some hard times.

Chapter 12

I have made this seem like a really sad job but believe me, there are normal times as well. There are moments that aren't so intense and… some that were actually comical. Some of the reasons that I listened to after a traffic stop were unbelievable and funny. For example; I was working radar one Saturday morning and it was a beautiful sunny day. My radar stated squealing and I looked up and saw a… mini- van, yeah a mini-van. I was working a 30mph zone and this little soccer mom van was running 60 plus mph. I pulled out and got behind the van and turned on my lights… then bumped my siren and the van pulled to the side. As I approached the driver's window, I could see through the mirror it was a female, probably in her forties and she was shaking her head back and forth like she was saying "No." She rolled her window down and she started saying, "I've told him a hundred times not to do this and now I am going to get in trouble." "I just can't believe this; wait until I see him." I asked for her license and insurance card and she handed me her driver's license.

I again requested her insurance card and she told me that she couldn't do that. I was a bit curious and asked her why not, and did she have insurance. She replied "Yes, I have but I can't show it to you or I will go to jail" I thought to myself… what the hell is she talking about. I told her she would have to explain and she started; "My husband and I are up here to visit our daughter. We went to the lake this morning (which would explain why she was in a bathing suit) and forgot towels. I was in a hurry to get back to the lake because we have to go back home today. I would love to show you my insurance card, but I've told my husband so many times not to do this and now I am in trouble." I stopped her and asked "What are you in trouble about?" She continued; "My insurance card is in the glove box under the passenger seat (remember those?) and my husband keeps a pistol in there. I am not going to open that compartment." I requested she step out of her vehicle and she did, wrapping a towel around herself. I went around to the passenger side and opened the glove box.

When I opened that compartment I saw a beautiful Browning Hi-Power handgun in a Browning holster. This was no normal handgun; it was an expensive gun in perfect shape. There was a map, some Kleenex, and an insurance card there as well so I removed the card. I walked back around the van and told her she could have a seat again. She was real quiet and finally ,"Are you going to take me to jail?" I answered, "For what?" She looked rather confused and wondered why I wouldn't arrest her for a handgun in the car. Truth is, I never cared if an honest good citizen carried a gun in the car for defense. On the other hand, I did care if a criminal or drug dealer carried one… period! I explained this to her and then started writing a speeding ticket. She seemed surprised about the ticket and asked, "Are you giving me a ticket?" and I replied, "Yes, ma'am, 60 in a 30 is just not negotiable." After signing the citation, I thanked her for cooperating and she drove off. I'm not sure, but I think she thought I might forget about the speeding, but hey… I enforce traffic laws, right? I have told this story for years and still catch myself grinning when I remember it.

Before I continue let me bring you up to date on my social and family life at this moment in time. Having Sunday off helped a lot towards spending time with the family. During the two years I was a traffic investigator, I was able to take some vacation time and got to take the kids to some interesting and fun places. We spent time at the "Deer Lease" if you recall reading about that. We even had time to take off so I would go on a Saturday as well to hunt with all my friends... Ol' Tall and Lanky, Marine Buddy, Banker Buddy, the Tush Hog (Chief of Police) and several other officers and friends. We were able to spend time at friends' homes for gatherings because by now all the friends had kids of their own so the parties had turned into a family occasion. We had purchased new ATV's and would just go up and ride sometimes. I was able to do both for now... work and home while enjoying both. We were even making time to go places with my in-laws and a trip to Virginia to see my Mom and Dad. That was a great trip and I'll never forget it. My boys actually became interested in the battlegrounds, Mt. Vernon the farm where Secretariat was born and trained on and of course... Busch Gardens and Kings Dominion (amusement parks) There was Virginia Beach, Jamestown and on and on. So many things to do and we tried to do them all. So needless to say the events in my life were looking good and all seemed well.

Back to some of the more humorous things that happened while I was on Traffic. I remember working at a double stop sign one day and very few people stopped at either one. For some reason folks just didn't want to stop at the signs so quite a few tickets could be written there most anytime, any day. I pulled a college student over for not stopping at both signs and when I got up next to her window I introduced myself and told her why I had stopped her. I then asked her if there was reason that she didn't stop... she was fidgety and said loudly, "I gotta pee. I just live up here. Please let me go pee and I'll take the ticket." Although I didn't laugh out loud, I told her to go ahead and stop next time. I would have never been able to write that ticket if she would have peed herself. I would have laughed too hard.

I was driving north on the main street through town morning and a little red car ran through a stop sign. It had come out of the Sorority Row area and I figured it was a student. I turned on the vehicle and when it pulled over; sure enough it was an SFA student. When I question her if there was an emergency she simply replied "No, I just didn't want to stop." I wrote her a ticket. The next day around the same time, guess what? Yep, her again at the same stop sign. After I wrote her for the second time, she stated that it was stupid to have a stop sign there and she wasn't going to stop. I know this is hard to believe but the next day was a carbon copy… another ticket. I explained to her that she had to stop or sooner or later she would have an accident. Never saw her again… maybe she got another color car. She did not contest it in court so I guess she paid the fines… don't know.

Another morning I was working radar on a long back street and my radar went crazy… 130 mph. This was in a 30 mph zone and I looked up to see a motorcycle coming towards me so I rolled the window down to hear the engine. Wow, he was flying and I hit my lights so he would start slowing down. The guy rode right up to my car and placed his bike on the stand as I exited. I questioned him something like… "Are you out of your mind?" He was grinning and I wanted to know what was so funny so here he went… "I just bought it last week and the salesman told me it would reach 120 mph in a quarter mile." Then he asked, "How fast was I going?" I replied to him he was traveling 130 mph and he was in a 30 mph zone. He was proud that the bike would do that and took the ticket. When he started to ride off, this idiot pulled a wheelie and was again speeding right in front of me. I motioned for him to come back and he did… another ticket but this time I informed him if he did anything while leaving this time I was going to hook him up. He rode off without further incident.

There were so many stories and so many excuses for traffic violations, I wish I had written them all down. I don't recall them all but I did let people slide on minor violation when they came up with a great excuse. The only place I wasn't flexible was in a school zone and I was serious about them. I set my own limits. For example; I would only pull over a speeder when they reached 13 MPH over the limit except in a school zone like I mentioned. So if you were traveling 40 mph in a 30 mph zone, chances are I wasn't going to pull you over. On stop signs, a person had to blatantly run it before I stopped them unless they almost caused an accident. I had to streamline things so I could keep up.

Mentioning the 13 mph brought back a weird memory, may I share it? I was instructed that there was a complaint in one of our north neighborhoods about speeding. I was to set up on the street and stay there until around 10:00 and only leave if I was called off. I got all set and turned on my handheld radar and within about fifteen minutes I had a 47 mph in a 30 mph… time to make a stop. I pulled the car over and while talking to the driver realized the he was the caller. This was the man that complained about other people speeding. While running his driver's license, I radioed my Sergeant to meet me after the stop and he did. After explaining to him what had just happened he told me to go ahead and leave the post and work traffic; we both laughed as we drove off.

I was moved to the evening shift for a week to participate in some sort of traffic specialty program. It was extra heavy enforcement but I can't recall what they called it. I was working traffic with the evening traffic units as well as filling in with a few patrol calls. One such call the first night was a family disturbance. We arrived at the residence to find a man and woman screaming at each other. Back then all that was done if nobody was hurt is separation for the night. Nowadays you can't do it that way but that was the practice then. The patrol officer took the man and I took the female and we divorced them for the night, although we normally made the man leave the house. They wanted it legal so we had them place their hands on our badge and made some gestures and they would separate for the night. I know it wasn't right but it was effective and nobody wound up in jail. It was changed because of statewide, not just in Nacogdoches, too many would return later and injuries and even deaths resulted. So to all of you that would argue and fight with your spouse, the reason you are arrested today is because of the action of the generation before you.

Drunk people… fraternity parties, they seemed to go hand and hand and we responded to a few along with noise complaints all night. We wrote PeePee tickets regularly… that's when someone urinates in public. Male or female, it didn't matter to them so it didn't to us. I have seen just as many women drop their pants and pee as I have guys. MIP tickets for those drinking underage which happened all the time. I arrested one guy who was peeing on the sidewalk and was intoxicated to the max. When I asked for his name or some Identification he told me he didn't have it on him… how about the name? He wanted to know my name so when I said officer Hensley he replied, " That's my name too, Officer Hensley" He then said, "You know you would've never known I was here if you weren't there." Okay, let's take a little trip.

During this enforcement period we worked all kinds of traffic problem areas and for long hours as well. The state had put into law that you had to carry proof of financial responsibility (Insurance Card) so a lot of citations were written when people didn't have them. We would set up stops where we had the drivers display a license and an insurance card. One night at North View Plaza, we were doing just that and if there was a violator they would pull to the right while they were written a citation. I will never forget that little light blue VW Cabriolet pulling over and I approached the driver's window. I got her license from her and started writing the ticket.

Another traffic officer (MY evening FTO actually) was walking up the passenger side of the car as I returned to the window as all the windows were down. I requested that she sign the ticket and she looked up at me and said, "Are you sure?" I was handing the booklet for her to sign and remember thinking, " Hell yes, lady, I'm sure, what kind of question is that?" When I looked at her before I spoke again… she had opened the front of her blouse, and pulled down her bra exposing her boobs to me. She said "Still want to give me a ticket?" It was hard to talk and I am sure I was every shade of red I could be, but I told yes she was getting a ticket and I said, "Now put those away before they get both of us in trouble." She laughed and told me that she had to try, signed the ticket and pulled away. The other traffic officer was laughing so hard he was in tears and at the end of the shift he let everyone at the station know about it too. I got teased for weeks over that, but I laughed with them because it must have been a funny sight.

Two of the traffic units were called to a wreck one of those nights and I was secondary so the other unit took lead. I went and positioned my car on a blind curve and turned on my overheads. The traffic was moving but slowly to get around the accident. Everyone was doing well until this one asshole drives up the shoulder of the road. There was nowhere for him to go, so he tried to get back in line but was forcing his way in. I walked down to where he was at and told him to hold up. I was going to get him back in line as soon as I could but he couldn't wait… so he pressed the accelerator and was headed right towards me. I was shining the light at and yelling for him to stop until finally I had no place to go. I threw the flashlight at the vehicle and broke the windshield and that got him to stop. Before the night was over, he had been charged with a DWI after being professionally removed from his vehicle (sucked out through the vent window) and I believe he resisted arrest, too!

There were many lighter moments, way too many to write in this and then there were the rewarding moments. I was working traffic of course, early one morning and that day had a rookie in training with me. I had become an FTO myself and did the traffic training during the day shift. Anyway we were set up in a school zone when a call came in about a possible bus accident. The shift Sergeant was very close and advised he would go see what it amounted to. A few seconds later we heard "204 to 207, I need you over here right now, hurry up" The sarge began calling in license plates and called in multiple wreckers and as I approached the scene I could see two badly damaged cars and a school bus on its side in a ditch. I stopped my car and let my rookie out and his instructions were do not let anyone down this road from this end. There was an intersection and he started routing them away. I called the sarge and asked him to stop traffic from the other side and reroute until further notice. Before I get into the accident let me say that rookie and my Sergeant did a hell of job keeping my scene intact for me.

I got to the bus and people were getting kids off the bus. They were being transported by ambulance and personal vehicles to the hospital for observation. I was looking for the driver and there he was, pinned under the bus... how the hell did he get there? The Fire department and EMT personnel freed him and he was okay, but scared as hell. Now for the cars and there were injuries in both vehicles. They were freed up and transported to the hospital so now it was time for me to take measurements and well you know the routine by now. At the hospital I got every name of every student and what seat they were sitting in, the driver's information and the occupants of the vehicles information and guess what... only two serious injuries consisting of a broken leg and jaw.

Can you believe that, such a bad wreck and all those kids and nothing more than some scratches and bruises and a car occupant with a broken leg, another with a jaw injury. The angels were looking down on those folk that day. It took seven pages to complete the report but it was complete by the following morning. The reward was afterwards in the following days... I received thank you cards from the parents of some of the kids along with the drivers of the vehicles. They wanted me to know how much they appreciated my handling of this situation. I saved those until my last move and somehow they were misplaced.

There were many accidents to work on dayshift, but there were also a lot of back up calls as well as being called as a primary officer on, well, anything! I received a call one morning about 8:00am to back up a patrol unit on a family disturbance call. The caller advised that there was loud yelling and crying coming from the next door neighbor's house. The patrol unit rolled up about the same time I did and the Sergeant also arrived. As we exited our vehicle we could hear screaming in the house. Everyone hurried up on the porch. This was a long narrow house and the layout inside was very different than most homes. The front door was located in the living room and then the rooms just sort of stacked on one another. From there you would enter a bedroom then another bedroom. After that was a bathroom on one side and dining area on the other. Finally, the last room in the house was a kitchen. As we approached the front door, I happened to look down and in behind a regular living room chair on the porch was a small child. This little girl could not have been more than two years old and… she had blood on her face. Her cheeks and lips were swollen and her eyes almost shut. I got on my radio and called for an ambulance, drew my weapon and prepared to go hunt the monster that would do this to a child. The patrol officer went in with me and the Sergeant stayed on the porch securing the child.

As we entered, we could hear the voices from the back of the house but had to slowly make our way through. The house was cluttered and we didn't want a surprise to jump out. Halfway through the living room, there was another child crouched behind a rocking chair… this one was maybe three at the most. He was in about the same shape as the little girl on the porch. The Sergeant had delivered the little girl to EMT personnel and had entered the house. He took the little boy out the door and we continued. The yelling had stopped or rather been muffled and now I knew it was coming from the next room, the kitchen. Only room for one officer at a time to enter this room so I went in first. I immediately saw a man with his arm around a woman's' neck and he started hitting her in the face with his fist. She was screaming and the faces of those kids went through my mind and… well… I went ballistic.

I could see he didn't have a weapon and there were none on a counter so I holstered my weapon and grabbed him by his wrist. I twisted him so hard I thought I had broken his arm… too bad I didn't. I looked in his eyes and yelled to him "Hit someone that will hit you back you piece of shit." This man attempted to hit me with his other fist and when he did I was able to force his head into the sink. Remember this was a very small space and there really wasn't a lot of room to be fighting in. I don't know what came over me, but the more he resisted the more I continued to shove his head in the sink. At some point, he stopped, struggling and the patrol officer was able to get handcuffs on him. I still had my hands on his head and my Sergeant placed his hand on my shoulder and said, "That ought to do it." I let go and walked behind them outside. They placed him in a patrol car and I walked over to the ambulance to check on those kids.

The lady was his wife and she was in really bad shape, but it wasn't something that time wouldn't heal, physically anyway. Those two kids, sitting there all beat up and bruised were a sight I will never forget. How could someone do this to a child? How could a grown man believe that a child could be so bad that they would deserve this treatment… how? By the time I was ready to leave, the EMT's had them laughing and smiling as they headed for the ER. I guess that I was raised very different than some. My own kids had acted up and done things they shouldn't have but I never struck a child for any reason. I never even spanked my kids… I know you don't believe that, but it's true. Their mother spanked them (not very hard), but I never did; you can ask them. It took a while for me to calm down after that but after an hour or two I got back to normal.

Chapter 13

To this day there are a handful of things that I still see in my mind and I guess I always will. There are times I will close my eyes and vision them; there are dreams about them and sometimes even nightmares. The two that stand out the most are the look in the eyes of the young man that died in my arms. I see those eyes in my dreams… it still hurts today. The look on the faces of those two kids that were so beat up… then the laughter as I was leaving letting me know that God was healing them. There is another time that the look of a person would stick with me for life; It all started on a chilly day before sunrise when that familiar sound "207, major 10-50, South at the loop" came across the radio. We were not quite through with briefing so I told the Lt. I would head that way and let them know what I needed. I arrived at the scene and I saw a truck hooked up to what was left of a travel trailer half in the street and half in a parking lot of a restaurant. As I got closer, I could see a mangled up mess of what was a car between the travel trailer and me. This accident had happened in the northbound lane so I went past it and came back to set up. I got my patrol car parked with overheads going and approached the car first. As I walked by that travel trailer I could not believe what I was seeing, it was like a tunnel had been bored through it. I got to the car to find several people from the restaurant were talking to a young woman pinned in the car. She was between the steering wheel and the driver seat and could not move. I started talking to her and she responded. I could hear the ambulance and Fire department on the way so I continued to talk with her to keep her calm.

She would sort of fade in and out and I could tell she was in a lot of pain and I kept talking to her. She started talking about her babies. "My babies are they okay?" I looked and didn't see anything in the passenger seat or rear seat. I asked, "Where are they?" and she replied, "In the back seat, find my babies." This car was really messed up and there was ripped sharp metal everywhere. I shined my flashlight in the rear floorboard and oh my gosh, there were two car seats upside down in the floor. The ambulance was still not quite there and then I saw it… one of the seats moved. I didn't know exactly what to do so instinct took over and I crawled into the back of that car. I don't know how I got through that entanglement of metal but I did and was able to reach the car seats. As I turned the first one upright… there was a tiny baby in it. This baby wasn't crying or fussing, this baby was sort of smiling (I'm told that is gas) and after I got that one upright I turned the next one over… another small baby… twins! This one was rubbing those beautiful eyes and then started to fuss a little.

By the time I had these two little ones out of those car seats some people from the restaurant had gathered around the car and the ambulance arrived with the Fire department. I don't remember in what order, I was busy at the time. I handed the children out of that spider web of metal to a lady and an EMT… now for me to get out. The Fire department was working on freeing the lady from the wreckage and I somehow got myself out of the back of that car. Well, I did have a little help from a firefighter, he bent a piece of that car so I could exit and I was thankful. I needed a minute before I was ready to work this accident so I was just standing there watching them free the lady... a tap on my shoulder. I turned to see an EMT who was a friend of mine and he quietly and calmly said "Come over here and sit on the back of the ambulance" I told him I was fine and needed to start my paperwork and he said "I think you have time for this, come on over here" I looked down and my arms were covered in blood, my blood. It had actually started to drip off my hands on to the ground. What the hell? Where did that come from? I walked over and sat down just like he told me to wondering how I didn't notice the bleeding until someone pointed it out.

He washed my arms off and there were tiny cuts everywhere. Nothing big or major, but like razor blade cuts on both forearms. He butterflied a few of the bigger ones and told me to drop by the hospital later on so they could check them out more. I agreed and after that I worked that scene. After I finished the wreck scene, I had to go to the hospital anyway to check on the car driver so I would go get checked out when I finished with her. I arrived at the hospital and was informed that the lady wanted to see me. She was in X-ray and as I walked in the room, she smiled at me. I got some information from her and checked with the hospital to find out that she should be fine. She motioned me over to her and when I was close she reached up, hugged me, gave me a kiss on the forehead, and told me thank you for helping her kids. Talk about something that made one feel proud... this was it. I watched her look of fear turn to relief and remembered one of the reasons I wanted to be a police officer.

My duty as a traffic investigator was coming to an end, but one more event would again be one of those memorable moments. I was at the station one day working on a report when the Captain walked in and started up a conversation. He advised me that some

University in Michigan wanted to use one of my accident reports in an instructional book on accident scenes. My first response was, "Is it the one on how not to do a report?" He laughed and told me that it was the fatality accident I had worked in front of the plywood plant, involving a log truck. This institute was impressed with the drawing I had completed as well as the overall report. I was happy that my work was so well received but that report belonged to the State of Texas so if they released it… so be it. I was still proud and requested a copy of the book once it was published. I could not tell you if it was ever published or not because I forgot about it and never received a copy, but it was an official letter I received from the institute in reference to the accident. So that would be some of the high and low points of patrol and traffic enforcement and now… I wanted to make detective.

I've written down a few things here to show you that a police officer is more that you think they are. We are people, plain ol' people that found a calling. We have feelings just like everyone else; we have emotions, just like everyone and we believe in what we do. Are there bad cops? Sure there are. Are there bad teachers? Of course there are. Are there bad bankers or bad businessmen and women? You bet. There are bad people doing everything in this world… there are bad preachers. Name a profession and there are bad people in them, that's our world we live in today and has been since forever.

I see or read so often that a certain group of people complain about being profiled or stereotyped and feel they are being mis-treated or even abused because of the situation. What makes police officers different? Our government people, the very ones we elect to an office to be our voice… are no longer our voice at all once elected. I belong to a motorcycle riding group, does that make me an outlaw

1% type biker? I have had people tell me that police officers are held to a higher standard... really? What standard is that? Who is responsible for those standards? Are my standards and yours the same? All officers came from a family and most have families of their own. Does the population of this country believe that a police officer is not proud and happy when they have a child? Do you think that they act different when they are able to buy a home or a vehicle? They act just like... well hell, a person.

Do police officers not feel sadness and hurt when they lose someone? Do they not celebrate birthdays or holidays like other people? What does the population think officers do? In a profession to help others at some point you have to take control. If you do not make your rent or payment, the bank does not just overlook it. They take some sort of action and in the end if nothing else works... foreclose. When an officer writes you a ticket, is that not a warning? If you step over the line and commit an offense against a person or society, you will most likely be arrested. So tell me what the difference is. Okay, I have preached long enough on this now, on with my story.

Chapter 14

An opening in C.I.D. was posted one day and I only had the minimum requirements to apply for it. I was up against several officers that were way more experienced than I and really didn't think I had a chance. I, with the help of an officer on my shift started preparing for the interview and evaluation. Part of the requirement was years of experience... 2 years minimum and that's what I had. This officer and I had become friends and she would go over things with me daily while there were slow moments. She came up with questions and situational events for me to answer or solve and then we would talk about it. Day after day waiting for the determination day to arrive, I read books and guides on how to handle crime scenes and interviews. Anything I could get my hands on to help me understand what was expected of a detective. Finally, the day arrived and I was called for my interview. I knew the answers for the questions asked and felt really good about the outcome of this interview. Once all the applicants had finished up it was hurry up and wait time. Later that afternoon it was announced and I didn't make it. I was told that I was in second place though and that these evaluations and interviews were good for a year so if something opened in a year I would have it. I learned that I had lost by two points. Each officer received a point per year of experience and the officer that beat me had four years... do the math. We basically tied until the years were added on. It was okay because I did that well and lost out to a really good officer that would become a friend as the years went by.

A Sergeant with the narcotics unit (it was referred to as the NED unit standing for Neighborhood Enforcement Division.) contacted me and asked if I was interested in joining his division. Basically it was the early stages of what would be called community policing. Since narcotics were probably my weakest area I thought… why not, it will help me keep advancing. I was now number 228. I had to attend several in service schools, but that was okay by me. I had always done well in these schools and as a matter of fact I was sent to schools by my Lt. to make sure other officers passed the classes. That was my objective… get certain officers through certain schools. I was pretty good at getting people to learn and maybe, just maybe, they were able to see my test answer sheet. I was now pushing three years as an officer and had several trainees under me already although it was for traffic we still had to answer those other calls. I felt that I was a good FTO and I think my trainees would mostly agree. Took a lot of extra time with my trainees to make sure they got as good of instruction as I did.

One of my trainees who is a respected detective today was great to train. One of the first days I had him with me we were sent to an alarm call at the bowling alley. We found an open back door to the machinery room and after drawing our weapons entered the building. I had requested radio silence so I could hear. As we made our way through that maze of equipment, we were being very quiet and listening for any noise. We were moving with him behind me and all of a sudden I heard the distinctive sound of a safety being released. Oh shit… he was behind me and "click" I continued on because I knew he was a good officer, but let's just say some things make your butt hole pucker up. This same officer during his ghost week got one of those raining, I'm in a hurry days. We worked wreck after wreck after wreck as fast as we could get to them… sixteen total for the shift. Most of them had no injuries so they were shorter but sixteen in one day is crazy. He completed eight of those by end of shift and only had one day left on his ghost period. Pending eight reports was unusual but we had to. He and his wife came by my house that night and he spent a couple of hours finishing them up… yes, sir he made a fine officer.

Anyway back to the NED unit… and remember this was a fore-runner to community policing. There were four officers in this unit and we all were fairly new at the positions. The sergeant had been there for years and yet he seemed lost half the time. Don't get me wrong, he was a great person just a little unorganized at times… well, most the time. This particular way of working was very different. Some days we rode bicycles down the historic scenic trail just to see who was walking it. We actually rode up on a drug deal one day… they never heard us approaching until we were right on top of them. Some days we went to the cinemas in plain clothes just to see who was going during the daytime and what was being watched. There were many days we rode around in plain vehicles to see who was out and about.

Other responsibilities were raiding drug labs although we only did one while I was with this unit. We worked a lot of evenings in and around Fraternity and Sorority parties with underage drinking. We had to draw up our own search warrants and make sure a judge would sign them and this was valuable for me later on down the line. We were the extra patrol some nights as we helped all the patrol units out and did many back up calls. On the brighter side, we also did a lot of public relationship work and were invited to many gatherings. Barbeques, parades, and just about anything going on at the Expo Center including Concerts were a place to be. I was able to see several entertainers while attending these. We also worked traffic on the loop and called it... interdiction! In today's world it would most likely be called profiling.

One night we pulled over a pick-up truck with a camper shell on it. After figuring out something wasn't right about the driver and his story we had a drug dog brought in. The dog alerted quickly and after a little searching and dismantling we found a false gas tank full of dope. The icing on the cake was the mattress in the back of the truck was stuffed with cash. I can't recall the amount but it was one or two hundred thousand dollars. We picked up weed on the loop regularly as it would come through in passenger vehicles, buses, semi rigs and any way they could carry them. On a stop one night, we had two motorcycles pulled over and couldn't find anything on them. I remembered one of my favorite movies, *Easy Rider*, so we opened the gas tanks. There it was in a plastic tube. I guess they liked the movie, too. You should have seen the faces of those guys when I asked them if they would really put in the tank... as they say, priceless.

One evening right before dark a car drove past us at around 80 mph. so we pursued it. After we got the driver to stop the Sergeant approached the vehicle while I was back up on the passenger side. He took a driver's license and a card from a rental car place in Houston and motioned me back to the car where the two other officers had parked as well. He said, "Y'all know who we got here?" Who? "We got Goose." What the hell was he talking about? "We got Goose?" "No, that is the guy that played Goose in *Top Gun*" "That's Anthony Edwards?" Yes, it was Anthony Edwards. So instead of writing a ticket to him he autographed one to the NED Unit. Seems he was on his way to film another movie, but anyway he headed on north.

My first drug raid was an interesting event and this is something else we did in NED. We wore all black with POLICE in white, mask included. The first time we entered a suspected drug house, I was the second in line carrying a shotgun. The breacher announced our presence and took out the door so now I was first in line. In I went where I saw several people start scrambling around. Constantly looking for a weapon but not seeing one, we got them on the floor and cuffed very quickly.

After the first one, it became about a once every two weeks thing. We were into something different all the time and one night on South59 was yet another drug bust. Another officer and I were in some woods across Highway 59 from an old run down motel. There was always quite a bit of drug traffic at the location and using a night vision scope borrowed from DPS we monitored this activity for a couple of nights. I made note of who was coming and going and the length of the visits. It was the first time I had ever used a night scope so it was cool to me. We would not take place in the actual raid but monitor everything and so that's what we did. The suspects in the room were so relaxed and had no idea that just around the corner the officers were staging the raid. We could see all of them from our vantage point. When those officers moved in it was a sight to see. It went mostly as planned and we made some arrests.

Then there were the jump out nights... yes I said jump out. I realize this worked at one time but this was the stupidest thing we ever did, whoever thought of this must have been on crack themselves. The Sergeant would go borrow a big box van or delivery truck from a rental place and drive around the high risk neighborhoods.

If he saw anything that looked suspicious, he would stop the vehicle and we would open the door and "JUMP" out of the back of the truck and start chasing people. What? Half the time we didn't even know who to chase but he liked doing it so… we kept on. We ran down this guy one night and after we had him stopped, you guessed it… he didn't have a damn thing on him.

This would happen many times and at a point I think the Chief stopped it. Nobody was happier than me! I didn't know how this was supposed to be close to community policing but as time went on we did start doing some preventative things as well. Times had changed and so did we… things would be different. I will say one thing about this unit; we were close and protected one another. That Sergeant was a good guy but got into a little trouble over alcohol later in his career and lost his job. He passed away a few years later after spending time in a nursing home and I still miss him, I liked him. He was replaced by another Sergeant and we continued with practices only a little more organized.

One Friday night in August 1993 while out working the area around the college, I got a call to report to the station. Once there I was told my wife had called and advised them that my father was having emergency surgery the following Monday. I called my mother in Virginia and she told me that the doctors believed he had a tumor in his colon and were going to try to remove it. When I got home a few minutes later, we loaded up the SUV and headed for Virginia. Twenty three hours and 1300 miles later, we pulled into their drive in Ashland, Virginia which is just north of Richmond. It was late and after some much needed sleep, we were informed of the events and actually understood what we heard. My dad looked tired and he appeared to have aged a lot of years since I had last seen him. His massive arms were smaller and honestly, there was no doubt he was sick, very sick. We spent Sunday talking and trying to get a grip on the situation. My aunt and uncle from Ohio arrived to help support us. One of my dad's cousins from Houston also showed up for support. My youngest brother was already living in Richmond, so he and his wife were there along with their new baby. We waited for Monday on pins and needles hoping and praying the doctors could do something for him.

We waited patiently in the hospital for hours to hear something on his condition. Finally the surgeon walked out and sat between my mother and myself. He explained that it was a tumor and it was cancer… it had spread into the lungs and liver. He told us there was nothing he could do but reroute the colon to give some relief. He said we could elect to try treatments, however, it was so very large and he didn't know that it would work. Damn… he just told us my dad was going to die. My mother wept while we tried to comfort her, but it didn't help. This was reality, this was happening to my dad and there was nothing I could do to help him, except comfort my family. I called my brother in Nacogdoches and explained to him to drop everything and get on the road to Virginia to ensure he would get to see Dad and him and his wife arrived the next day.

We were all able to spend some time with him for a few days before everyone had to head back home. He was able to go home before we left, but there was one thing… while he lay in that hospital and joked with all the nurses he seemed at ease, not happy, at ease. He motioned me over when he and I were the only ones there and had me lean down to hear him and he said "Don't bury me here; I want to go home to Texas. Take your mother home to Texas too, all of her friends are there… you take care of her." "Will you do that for me?" and I said "Yes ,Sir, I will." One of my cousins showed up and also helped comfort us and we were very appreciative of that because everyone was so tired and wore out.

It was time for my wife and I to go back to Nacogdoches and when I told my dad goodbye I knew in my heart it was final. I knew I would never see him alive again. I cried as I drove towards Texas and thought of the great things he did over the years for me and others… those thoughts helped me cope with his illness. We kept in contact by phone daily and I was always praying for a miracle, but on October 19, 1993, a few days before my birthday, my little brother called and informed me we had lost our father' he was only 57 years old. I just sat down in a rocking chair and stared off unfocused and rocked back and forth for a while.

My family members were calling and at one point I couldn't talk to them so my mother and father-n-law took the calls. I had to go tell my two boys now. That turned out to be one of the hardest things I ever did. They thought their Grandpa could walk on water. We arranged to fly to Washington D.C. one way so we could drive my mother back to Texas. She made funeral arrangements in Richmond for the friends he had made there and the following day my wife and I were headed for Virginia. We were picked up by my younger brother. We made it to my mother's house and broke down again. The services were later in the day and when we arrived at the funeral home there were a lot of people there. The first thing I did was walk to the casket with my mother then I cleared the room and just me and my dad had one last talk… I was okay from then on. The service was beautiful and then the funeral home transported him to Texas. My wife, brother, sister-n-law, mother, and I headed for Texas in my folk's van. On a brighter note, we did stop at a Cracker Barrel and celebrated my birthday on that trip. To this day I love to celebrate birthdays for everyone, but my own just doesn't mean much to me anymore.

The trip was okay, long and tiring and we all knew once we were in Nacogdoches, we had another service to go through. I don't mean that badly, it's just we all said goodbye in Virginia. And so it was… a very large service and the chapel was packed, not even standing room was available. My cousin that had come to Richmond when he was sick did the sermon and he was wonderful. Nobody could have done better; he had known his uncle all his life so I considered him an expert. A close friend of mine sang "How Great Thou Art" and yes, he did a wonderful job. Friends from Houston were there and so many people he had worked for and had worked for him and… you know what? He was still my hero. The service was beautiful and at the end as they were removing the casket to the vehicle, I looked up and there were shoulder to shoulder police officers on both sides crossing Highway 259 to the cemetery across the street. All four lanes and the turning lane were covered… wow, tell me again how there isn't a brotherhood among officers. I am grateful today for what those officers did. After the service we all tried to get back in a life routine. We did get my mother moved back to Texas and I was going to keep my word and promise I made to Dad about taking care of Mom… period!

Now back on the job, the NED unit had started to concentrate on narcotics. We made some strides and some good arrests but you know you take one down and two pop back up… or it seemed that way. We started working mostly nights so I was again not at home with my family. At least I had nearly every Sunday off so there was a complete day with them. My boys were growing up so fast, seems like they moved from tricycles to four wheelers overnight. At this point I was enjoying getting the dope off the streets, but I didn't care much for the narcotics division. It wasn't the people at all, it was the type of work… some officers are made for it and some aren't. A change was on the horizon and it would come as a surprise. Remember when I was beat out of C.I.D. by a more experienced officer… he was resigning to go to work for the County Attorney and it was less than a year since we tested. What this meant to me was that I was going to C.I.D. very soon.

Chapter 15

As the days wound down for me in NED, I was assigned less and less so I would not have a huge carryover when I transferred. I started doing much of the paperwork as opposed to field work. It seemed that those days of waiting took forever but finally I was informed to report to C.I.D. the following morning and to wear slacks, a coat and a tie. I had a detective that was going to start training me and would spend time with all of them over the next few weeks. I was excited about the move and after all this was my dream job. I would be off on weekends unless called out and work 8:00 am until 5:00 pm unless something happened that would cause me to stay after. I would be able to spend time with the boys… the Junior High aged boys, most of whom do not want to spend time with their parents. Had I failed again? I would now have a take home car, something I had not had since my dad gave me one in the masonry business. I was the proud driver of a "Shamu" that was what the Chevrolet Caprices looked like then and my number would be 318. I was ready to start, oh and by the way… remember that officer that responded to the nightclub, the one I said was the shortest cop I ever saw? The one that was calling the shots that night… remember him? He was my new boss, he was the C.I.D. Lieutenant. So away we go!

My first day and it was spent getting to know everyone better as well as getting started on what a detective did. I spent the first day with the Sergeant and he walked me through many of the procedures.

He gave me a pager (remember there were no cell phones just huge bag phones) and told me that while I was training, I would be on call with each detective. Being on call… I thought that sounded cool but it was in fact a pain in the ass. For those who do not know about "On Call Status" allow me to explain; it meant that any after-hours call went to you and you had to stay in town and be available for those calls. The week prior to being on call you were responsible for filing all misdemeanor cases with the County Attorney. You had to be available for phone calls as well, just in case an officer needed a question answered on a scene or whatever reason.

As a detective, you didn't receive any compensation for this time even if you had to work an extra 30-40 hours in a week, no compensation. No compensation for having to stay at home and be ready either… you got your pay. The pay was the same as a patrol Sergeant pay except a patrol Sergeant got overtime and comp time. Nowadays it is much different and our detectives are compensated for their time, but then you just gave it up… and didn't complain. I was again the rookie of the bunch and trust me when I tell you they teased me a lot. It was, however, all in fun and I found them an easy bunch to work with.

These guys were very different from other officers and each other. First of all there was the Lt; Feisty and cursed constantly and didn't really care who heard him. He was an aggressive detective in his younger days and expected you to work your ass off for him. He always wanted to look good to the top administrators especially on statistics. He had a short fuse and a fast temper and liked to close his office door and prop his feet on his desk while he drank his morning coffee. You always had to be careful what you said and how you answered him… he would jump down your throat in a heartbeat. I don't believe he was afraid of anything and would take the lead on a situation if one paused too long.

Then there was the Sergeant… a country boy if there ever was one. Cowboy boots, handlebar moustache… looked like he was out of the old west and talked it too. A Slow Texas draw made conversations with him take a while but he was alright and had been an officer for a long time as well. He would assign the cases to the other detectives and hold the morning briefings.

Next was another seasoned officer that had wanted to be a cop all his life. A well respected detective and also was the representative for the Crime Stoppers organization in Nacogdoches. I had known him prior to working for the department and got along well with him. I still have much respect for him today, hell I have respect for all of them. After him was another seasoned officer that I had heard stories about for a while. This man was sort of a loner but did a very good job investigating just about anything. He was intelligent, but he was different. We became friends and worked cases pretty quick even though he would rather do things alone. I learned a lot from him.

Then last but not least… there was my main trainer… the other half of the MP's. Again, allow me to explain. While doing my training I was working with all of the detectives, learning something from each of them. After a short period I was placed with this detective primarily. Next to me he was the baby detective and… well let's remove the Lt. because he stayed in his office so there were five of us. Three of the guys were tall and my trainer and I were, for lack of a better word… let's just say short. One day, my trainer and I were at his desk going over some sort of paperwork and we overheard the Sergeant say over the phone… "Do you want one full size detective or two half size detectives?" What? Half Size? Us?

Apparently the caller wanted two half-sized ones so the Sergeant while trying not to laugh said," I'm sending the MP's right now. No, I don't mean Military Police, I mean Midget Patrol." Today that would be wrong and we would have to be the Mini Patrol or something, but then it was okay and it stuck... and stuck... and stuck. We were the MP's from then on and still have people refer to us as that twenty years later... wow, right? We were a motley crew but an effective one and I was learning the whole time.

My first call on my own was a death scene and even though it's not funny at all, the way it came about was. There was a house that flies had covered up and for anyone who never smelled what a decaying human body was like, well it's got to be the worst smell ever and I have thrown away several nice sport coats and ties over the years. It's very distinctive and so it was known there was a body in this house. The house was locked up so the patrol officer had to break in and immediately called in C.I.D. I responded as I was supposed to and when the other detectives were satisfied that is was a natural death they left laughing... leaving the rest with me. Whew... stink, stink, stink... so bad that a patrol officer had to excuse herself to go outside for a breath of fresh air. I asked her if she smoked and when she said she did, I told her to have a cigarette before she came back in. I had been on death scenes before from natural to suicide. Some were bad and some weren't as bad. There were those times that most of the victims head was missing and pieces of people everywhere from a powerful gunshot to someone who looked asleep.

Let me fill you in on this one; a male was lying on the floor of his living room naked. There was a telephone table that was knocked over on its side and a telephone on the floor. There was a full tub of clean water in the bathroom along with two gas space heaters burning wide open. The victim had a gash on the back of his head. So imagine this body had been here a few days and basically slow cooked in that heat. What do you think happened? All the doors were locked from the inside with a hasp type lock and the windows were secured. Well, figured it out yet? Let me help you... This man had run his bath water and about to get in the tub when the phone rang. It was in the winter time so the heaters were on to warm the house. Upon examine the table which was square, small amounts of hair and tissue were found so... got it yet? Continuing on, he slipped or tripped and fell striking his head on the table falling to the floor either dead then or unconscious and died later. All the pieces of that puzzle fit together nicely so do you think that's what happened? After a full investigation, that is what we believe happened, but this is how you think while looking at a scene.

Shortly after I made it to C.I.D., the detective in charge of the Crime Stoppers program left for the newly formed Nacogdoches Independent School District Police Department. It was formed partly because of a gun call on one of the campuses where a shot was fired. I was chosen to fill his shoes with Crime Stoppers and quickly moved up to number 317. Let me tell you those were some big shoes to fill because he had done an outstanding job with the program. I would be on television, in the newspaper and on radio on a weekly basis and it all seemed great except that I was told not to let it interfere with my caseload. I'll be damn, I just took more time away from my family. I look back sometimes and wonder what I was thinking at times. Anyway, during the day I spent most of my time working cases and then in the afternoon I worked on Crime Stoppers. Work a rape... film a TV spot. I will say this, it kept me very busy.

I recall a case I had where someone had shot up an area of town with an SKS or AK. The Lufkin Police had arrested a male subject for doing something very similar about an hour after ours had occurred. Lufkin also had a juvenile in custody that we needed prints off of and so I drove to Lufkin. I went by Juvenile probation and printed the suspect, then I went to the Police Department to talk with this shooter they had. It was funny in a way… he was brought into a room where I was and he sat down across from me. I started getting out my note pad from my folder and the print card was on top of it. I placed the print card on the table while I pulled out the pad and the whole time he stared at it… really hard. I put the print card back in my folder and started talking with him. He didn't answer so I asked if he wanted to talk, he had been read his rights. He looked at me with a poker face and said, "You already know I did it. You got my prints and you know so I will just tell you." He gave me a full confession of the shooting in Nacogdoches, even though I informed him that the prints had nothing to do with him. Pretty crazy but shit like this happened all the time. I think to be a good detective means to let them talk and you do the listening. Criminals love to brag so I always let them… all they wanted.

Being in a college town you can imagine that we had our share of sexual assault complaints. Any that occurred on campus were investigated by the University Police but off campus were ours. There were several complaints over the years and most were legitimate claims, however, there were the ones that were bullshit. For example… I was called out at around 4:00am one morning to a sexual assault (rape) victim at the emergency room. I arrived and after the doctors and nurses were finished up I started to interview the young lady. She seemed like a normal teenager, but I believe she was twenty years old. She explained to me that a guy she didn't really know had invited her and her friend over to his apartment that night and after a few drinks her friend left. She stayed and decided that had too much to drink and she would just sleep on the couch.

Without going into great detail, I'll tell you that the two had sex and she stated she didn't want to. She advised he forced her to have sex and she wanted to file charges. This wasn't my first rape and something just didn't seem right about it so I told her to go home and get cleaned up or whatever she wanted to do and meet me at the station later to complete the report. She complied and was there within a short time frame. I questioned her again and her story of the events had changed. She informed me that her father was on his way from Houston and he was upset. She asked me what could happen to the suspect if this continued and I told her he could go to prison but if he did rape her then he deserved it. She began to change up a lot then and her story started to get really unorganized. We continued to talk and she finally broke down in tears and said. "I am so sorry, I lied to you. I do not want that boy to go to prison."

This young lady broke down and told me that she had consensual sex with the boy, but was afraid her boyfriend in Houston would find out and came up with this story to protect herself because they used no protection. Wow... all that, really? She was willing to possibly send a young man to prison and have him registered as a sex offender for the rest of his life to save face... wow! Her father arrived a little later and, of course, being the father, he wanted to get his hands on this asshole that raped his daughter. Most parents would react the same way and did. I told him very calmly that before he made any threats he needed to speak with his daughter and provided them a private office to do so. Within ten minutes her father exited the room and told me he was sorry for the trouble his daughter had caused. He wanted to know if any charges were going to be filed on her and I told him none were. He then stated "You won't have to worry about her anymore here, I am taking her home to go to school there and she has a lot of explaining to do with her boyfriend" He thanked me again and they left the station. Please understand again, there were real rape cases and we worked hard on them and made arrests but this one stood out to me.

I was working a burglary case I was called out on one time and had the suspect at my desk and talking. He was reluctant at first but as we continued he loosened up and sort of started bragging about his accomplishment. We had agreed that the truth was the best thing and all that was needed was a written statement from him as to what had happened. He agreed but wanted to use the restroom and have a cup of coffee first. I escorted him to the facilities and got him a cup of coffee and then we went back in the office. He was about ready to start writing his statement and my Lt. walked in. Soaked because of heavy rain, he was not a happy camper. As he walked pass the defendant he said out loud something to the effect of the defendants status and did we have enough to put him in the mother-effin joint. Really? That guy looked at me and shoved the pen and papers at me and told me where to stick them. I actually got a conviction on that case but had to put in a lot of extra work but hey… that was the Lt. Had to love him!

My Crime Stopper's position was coming full circle now and being very successful. Our program started to receive state awards for productions and statistical gains. In a few short years it grew from an already good program to a state recognized program. Nine state awards in six years. I would love to take the credit for that, but it was way more than me. There were hours and hours of volunteer work put in by board members to make it a success. The president of this board was my old friend... remember Banker Buddy from the deer lease? The members backed me 100% and helped in any way I needed to forward this program. Over all my years I never worked with a greater group of volunteers.

The fund raisers, the advertisement, the commercials, all the little give away items (hats, key chains, golf tees, pens, pencils... you name it) they approved of were a huge part to the success. A crawfish boil and live band... for free. That's right because Lufkin had a band consisting of police officers that happened to be musicians or maybe it was the other way around. Regardless of what they were, they were good and helped us on several occasions. What a group of wonderful people everyone involved with Crime Stoppers was. I traveled to state conventions always accompanied by at least one or two board members some times more. We received more compliments than should be allowed; again I credit it to the wonderful board. These guys gave me a watch when I left the program a few years later; I still have and cherish it. I think some of the best times I experienced as an officer were with Crime Stoppers. I made lifelong friends with so many people from all over the state.

There were the dark days in C.I.D. as well, and I hesitate to write them down because I don't want to offend anyone, but this is how it happened. One thing I never understood was the fact that since I became a police officer, I was labeled a racist... why is that? I have thought back and for the life of me can't remember arresting a single person because they were a certain color. I can't remember the arrest and filing charges on anyone because of their religion or where they are from. Not one time did I charge anyone with being gay or poor or rich or any other reason that has to do with anything other than the fact… they committed a crime. I arrested criminals because they needed to be arrested and prosecuted. I have arrested murderers, thieves, rapist and dope dealers but always because of the action they committed and not for any other reason. I looked up the definition to criminal and nowhere does it mention a race or color or national origin or even religious belief. So because I am white, a male and a police officer then that makes me a racist. I'm sorry but I need an explanation… that doesn't compute well.

I have been told so many times the only reason you arrested me is because I'm black or because I'm Mexican (not Hispanic) and the fact is… it's just not true at all. If you ask me if there are racist police officers, my answer is yes but… on the same note are there racist preachers? Answer is also, yes there are. Anyone can be racist if they choose to be and whether it's right or wrong is up to you. Prejudice is another word used often with police officers and again I answer this; everybody dislikes something in the world and everybody doesn't believe in every belief in the world. Do you know someone who loves everyone? Really, because I believed Jesus was waiting in Heaven. What I'm trying to get across is the world is full of prejudice people and some of them are police officers but stop and ask yourself "What are they prejudice against?" Personally I am prejudice against criminals that prey on the elderly and young. Could that be why I try to prevent it? What are you prejudice against? There is something there if you are honest with yourself.

Another detective and I once made an arrest of four individual teens that had attacked and robbed a couple while they were walking along a scenic trail. This trail runs through Nacogdoches and is noted attraction to the town. The male of the couple was injured and all of the money, credit cards along with the wallet were taken.

When the four were brought in for an interview they all had different responses to question of why they committed the offense. The best I remember was that two denied they were involved even though the other two placed them there along with the victims. The others told me that they did it because the couple was white and they deserved it. Really? Would it shock you that we were denied to file this as a hate crime? Why you ask… because the victims were white. Just one more of many questions I have for the system… what the hell?

Anyway, I have gotten off track and need to get back to my story of the darker side of law enforcement. I have known over my career several officers that would steal things, some were alcoholics and even some that used drugs. I felt they should find a new profession and sooner or later, most were forced to. I knew an officer that cheated an insurance company (pure fraud) and got away with it, but he is no longer an officer. As much as I dislike insurance companies, they are a necessity in this country. I know an officer that got a DWI… but he is not an officer anymore either. So there is dark side to law enforcement but they are people just like everyone else… full of flaws. There have been bad cops since cops began, but most of them and I mean most of them really care and that's why they do the job. And… I am a Christian so I believe there was only one perfect person that ever walked this earth, the rest are regular people. I will stop the preaching now and end this chapter short.

Chapter 16

Some of the other cases worked in C.I.D. were a walk in bank robbery and a drive through bank robbery. The first one happened at a bank on University Drive across the street from the post office. Next to the post office is a large patch of thick woods with a creek running through it. It borders the SFA stadium parking lot. A young man entered the bank and made the clerk believe he had a weapon. Once he got the money he ran into the wooded area across the street. The Police departments from Nacogdoches City and SFA responded and so did C.I.D. It really didn't take long to apprehend the suspect because he got himself turned around in those woods and wound up in a swampy area where he got himself stuck... from the minds of babes!

The other one I remember was at the drive through where a driver of a vehicle displayed a gun and scared the clerk into sending him the money through the vacuum tube. A crime stopper tip led to clearing of this one... dumb ass forgot there were cameras on every drive through so his picture was easy to show on television. Many, many, times we made our cases just by being patient and watching for their mistakes. During this period our Sergeant left to go to the Sheriff's Office and my little partner became the new Sergeant. I was now number 316. We welcomed a new member in a patrol corporal who was young, aggressive, highly intelligent and a lot of fun to be around. He would soon be partnered up with me.

There was a problem though, he wanted more and had his sights set on the FBI. We did become fishing partners along with some other police type people.

The Chief of Police, the Chief of the School Police, the assistant Chief, the city Detective that went to the school, the County Attorney, a city manager, my partner and I made up a fishing club. It was a lot of fun and we held our own tournaments. Trophies were bought and given out for most fish and biggest fish. It was a way to unwind a little and we took advantage of it as often as we could. All the gatherings took place on private property and we fished the same lake every time. We would pair up and hit the water... well it was like a regular tournament, but we made all the rules, some as we went along. We would consume some adult beverages and had cook outs... these days were something to look forward to. I'm not sure what happened but we slowly stopped getting together and eventually the Alazan Sportsman's Society or "ASS" as we called it ceased to be. I truly miss those days

There was a time during this period that the department sort of went to war with itself... let me explain. For some reason there was, for lack of a better term... a power struggle between patrol and C.I.D. I don't know what caused it or who caused but somehow it happened. Patrol was to call out a detective when they needed one after hours. We were getting call out for some non-emergency situations. In other words, we were being called for things that would normally wait until we got to work. The detectives were working lots of hours of overtime and remember there was no compensation. The top dogs of both divisions were at it over this, our Lt. claiming that the supervisors didn't need to call on certain things and the other Lt.'s claiming they did. It got so bad that some of the detectives placed recorders on their home phones to get what the shift supervisors were saying on tape.

I promise I never wanted to be in the middle of one of these squabbles, but it happened anyway. The Sergeant of our division decided that when one of us was called then we called him to determine if we responded. Keep in mind that this was only on questionable calls. One night I get a call… the caller I.D. showed from the station so I started my recorder. I was told that Patrol had found an abandoned vehicle with the wheels taken off. They weren't sure, but they wanted to check the trunk and wanted me to come to the scene. I told them to stand by and I called my Sergeant and advised him of what they wanted. His response was to tell them to open the trunk and if they found something illegal or a body then call back and we would respond. Otherwise they could have the car towed. I called patrol back and told them that and they said okay then… your call. To make a long story short, it was a mistake because that abandoned car eventually led to a murder charge and arrest. It worked out, but not in a desired way. I hated I was a part of that and yet I was certainly glad we got the perpetrator. I still have that tape today… kept a hold of it for proof and I am glad that the recorder was there.

I was sleeping away one 4th of July night when my phone rang. It was the Sergeant on duty at the station and he is one of those slow talking Texans that doesn't get too upset over much. He said to me " Hey Kenny, we got ourselves a murder or that's what it looks like… we got one juvenile in custody and need you and Technical Services to come on out" I told him I would be on my way and called the TSD officer as I left the house. We arrived at the scene to find the deceased victim lying in a driveway with what appeared to be a stab wound to the chest and in to the lungs. The shift was short that night as well and many people were starting to gather around the house, angry people! The officers formed a perimeter for us as we worked the area.

I called for a Justice of the Peace and she arrived shortly after. This was her first murder as she was a new JP, but she treated it like she had been doing this her entire life, so professional about everything. The crowd learned that the juvenile suspect was in a squad car and started throwing bottles and rocks at us. They were cursing us and we didn't know why. The mother of the suspect arrived and had to be held back and the crowd got even angrier. Then... it all came together... the victim was in fact the suspects' father. I had another detective called in to help me out and had the suspect taken to the station and out of the area and that seemed to settle the crowd down. Handling juveniles is a totally different animal than adults, but we got a conviction and the juvenile was handled through the state.

We brought in a new detective after my partner was accepted to the FBI academy and ended his police career. I was happy for him but sure enjoyed working with him. The new guy was my old dayshift Sergeant and I already knew he was good to work with. As he was getting settled in the department, we started up a Citizens' Police Academy to help the public understand what we did. I was chosen to help out so I became a part of the staff. This organization met one night a week and to be honest it was fun. I was in charge of the crime scene and investigation night and had a part of a night to explain how Crime Stoppers worked. So what was I doing now? Being a full time detective, a coordinator for Crime Stoppers and a staff member for the Citizens' academy... again I forgot about my family. The tension around my house was growing and I was too blind to see it. Everything was work, work, work. I had become a workaholic. Funny how life just goes around in circles… this was the life I wanted away from.

I have to bring this up and again it is a low point… I got a call one night and the caller i.d. showed it was from the home of the Chief of Police. I was trying to get myself awake and knew I wasn't on call so why would he be calling me at this hour? I answered the phone and he told me we had lost a friend in a car wreck. It was Ol' Tall and Lanky, our hunting buddy. Damn… He wanted me to meet him at the accident scene and I got dressed and met up with him. We walked it and studied it trying to understand and I think, cope with the tragedy. Another friend lost, another sad day. Within a few years I would lose several friends including Banker Buddy and a college friend to cancer. My grandmother, well just like all people and families we were losing, it hurts. At one point I was afraid to make a friend… sounds silly, but I felt it none the less. Somehow we got through the days.

My friend of years, the Chief, decided it was time to retire and he did… I was happy for him and sad at the same time. I think he was a great Chief of Police. He would stand up for his men if they were in the right. He didn't care who liked it or not. He was for his department, he was a leader. Some didn't like that he was behind in modern equipment for the department but he was old school and thought hard work could get the job done. I admired and respected him and still do today. Most of us thought the assistant chief would be next but the city hired an outsider, a head hunter, to clean up the department which wasn't a mess! There were some other retirements that took place and some personnel changes. I don't know for sure, but I believe they were sort of forced. This new chief was not a bad person, but one day while out on the back step he started asking me questions. He wanted to know things about the city… and then he started telling me what they promised him. Why was he telling me this? I don't know, but I told him not to place too much stock in anything he was promised. I had seen what the city government did to people and I didn't trust most of them as far as I could throw them. And I'll say it… most of them were a bunch of lying bastards.

One of the great things about being an officer is all the in service training involved. The governing agency for Texas Peace Officers requires so many hours of in service training to keep one's certification. There are certain required courses to obtain higher levels and every two years certain courses are mandatory depending on what level and officer is at. There is a Basic, Intermediate, Advanced and Master Peace Officer levels and all this training gets you there. I have so many certificates of training I keep them in a large box. Some of the cool ones are; Forensic Hypnosis, Hostage Negotiator, Police Instructor, Firearms Instructor, Crime Scene Investigations, Death Scene Investigations, Sexual Assault and Child Abuse investigations and many others. I took all the required courses until I received my Master Peace Officer rating and these days I only have four hours of legal update every two years that are required. The rest can be anything I choose. I was able to have a little fun with the hypnosis information. After I returned from the training the new Chief wanted me to demonstrate my abilities. He knew I scored well in the class and he wanted to see it work. I got a volunteer… my Sergeant (I know, I was laughing too) was told he was the volunteer. I handed him a driver's license and told him to read the number on it and then took it away. This was around 9:00 am. I waited until around 3:00 pm and had him come to the interview room. The Chief, Assistant Chief and I were in the room. He sat down and was asked to tell us the number of the driver's license… he strained and tried but could not remember the number, not even close. So now it was time to see if I truly learned something from my week long 55 hour course I had taken.

I slowly and steadily took him through the steps of going under hypnosis. It took only a few minutes before he was so relaxed he was drooling and I had to tell him to swallow. I did this after we all smiled and grinned at each other (I know it wasn't right but it was sure funny and the Chief could hardly control himself) I instructed him how to recall his memory and pushed a piece of paper towards him. I gave him a pen and at the right time I instructed him to write down the license number he saw earlier in the day. He began to write down numbers and when he finished, I slowly brought him out of his relaxed state. Once back to normal I had the Chief compare the license and the paper… the numbers were the same, it had worked and my new Chief was impressed. All credit goes to the DPS instructor that I had in Austin, he was hard but one hell of a teacher. I was also able to use this skill to help college students with exams. It wasn't cheating in any form because you can't recall something if you never took the time to learn it. You could not remember something you never saw. I also was able to use this in helping witnesses recall plate numbers; however, it was never used in court due to all the loopholes with the theory.

I was helping with the explorer post at this time too. The explorers were young, mostly high school students that were interested in law enforcement as a career. I know… I was real smart when it came to police work, but real stupid when it came to family bonds. My boys had become grown and I missed too much of their childhood… I would pay for that move later. But for now I was helping these youngsters to learn about my profession. I helped the coordinators with techniques on building searches and traffic stops and of course, crime scenes. These kids would go to competitions and were pitted against other explorer posts. One such trip, my wife and I were invited to go on a trip with them. The idea was for me to hypnotize them the night before and hopefully they would remember what to do during the competition. It was a relaxing trip and we were furnished a room.

We all went out to eat some dinner and when we returned the coordinators had them assemble in one room. I explained to them what I was going to do (we had already cleared with their parents) and then requested the coordinators step aside and behind me. All eyes were on me and I begin the process. Slowly I brought each student to a relaxed state of mind and within about five minutes all the students, every single one was in a hypnotic state. The coordinators were amazed and walked among them checking on them. I instructed them how to recall what they had been taught and… slowly brought them all out. The signal I gave them was if they couldn't remember something to rub their index finger and thumb together until they recalled what they were searching for. All through the day you could see those kids rubbing the finger and thumbs together and then see the light bulb go off in their eyes as they recalled. Was it a success? They brought home 23 trophies from that competition so yes, I think it was a success.

We added a new detective to the gang and he was an ex-NED officer. He and I were , well we were acquaintances and I'm not sure we ever were actually friends. We went through some changes and some were for the good and some were not. I found myself once again, physically and mentally exhausted. I still loved my job but I was out of gas. The rolls of detective, Crime Stopper Coordinator,

Citizens' Police Academy Assistant Coordinator and helping out the Explorers were just too much.

I was spending at least twelve hours a day at work or doing something work related and most days more. Tension was building between my wife and I and I barely knew my two boys one of which had graduated High School. Where did the time go? Why did I spend it the way I did? I had no answers and decided I needed to speak with the Chief about reducing some hours. I didn't want to make him mad or have him think I was a quitter. I wasn't a quitter and I couldn't say no and that was partially to blame for my situation. Our Lieutenant retired and the Sergeant moved up and most of the detectives applied for the Sergeant position. Prior to me going to my interview I was informed that if I made Sergeant I would have to give up my role with Crime Stoppers. I didn't understand that because most of it was taken care of on my time and didn't cost the department much of anything. I was at a crossroads and had to do some serious thinking about that trade off. Being a Sergeant didn't mean that much to me, but Crime Stoppers was a state recognized success and I was part of the reason why.

One day the new detective and I were out in my unmarked vehicle checking on a few leads we had received. We were traveling northbound on University drive when all of a sudden a pick-up truck pulls out of a side street in to oncoming traffic from both ways. This truck darted across four lanes of traffic and the southbound vehicles came across into my lane headed right for me. There was a vehicle in the far right lane that kept me from moving over… there was no place to go. I applied my brakes extremely hard and the car started to skid and slow down. The oncoming vehicles… one swerved around me and back in their own lane while the other stopped straight in front of me about fifty feet. The car beside me stopped beside me and the truck that caused all this continued to drive on. Just as we got stopped, the brakes were still applied… BOOM from behind. It moved my car within a few feet of the vehicle stopped facing me in my lane. I looked in my rearview mirror and saw nothing but grill. I was putting the car in park and the other detective jumped out to try to get close enough to the pick-up to read the plates but was unsuccessful. I met the driver of the semi and being a cop said "Are you okay?" It was a mess and so we had to call in DPS since a police vehicle was involved. The other vehicles had left the scene while we were checking on everyone and now only the semi and we were left. The trooper was doing his traffic accident report and both the other detective and I were starting to hurt a little. I don't know if we were so pumped up we didn't notice or what but both of us were sore around the shoulders and neck area. The trooper questioned me if I was injured and I replied no, not really because I didn't think I was. The driver of the semi was so apologetic and I know he didn't do this on purpose and I assured him everything would be okay then the DPS trooper issued him a ticket for failure to control speed. I felt bad for the guy, but the trooper wrote the ticket to him.

What followed was two years of hell from an insurance company. I have always thought that people who claimed "whiplash" were full of shit. I laughed at them at times and never believed that such a thing really existed. I figured it was a way to screw an insurance company so people took advantage of the situation to do just that. Until this happened… I was wrong! I wound up at the ER that night with severe pains in my neck and shoulders. Sharp pains that Aleve wouldn't take care of. They took x-rays and referred me to my doctor the following day for treatment. After seeing my doctor, I was referred to a spine and neck specialist and spent several visits to his office. He was thinking a surgery was needed but the insurance company in all their wisdom decided no.

So I hired an attorney, I was tired of the insurance people calling the shots. I was eventually sent to a pain management doctor and he advised that he wanted to do a procedure to numb the nerves to stop the pain while the injury healed. I was all for that except the insurance company would only authorize the recommended procedure half way. By this I mean that this doctor wanted to perform the procedure on both sides of my neck but the insurance company would only allow one side. After several attempts by a good doctor and physical therapy, I was still in pain. The insurance company was denying treatments now and everyday was a war for me. All I wanted was to stop hurting… I had bills to pay and due to some circumstances, my mother was in need of financial help. I could not stop working… who was going to take care of everything? I finally told the attorney to get something done.

It took over two years of being called a liar and thief before it was brought to a table for settlement. Here I was sitting there after working all night at Wal-Mart on security and about to fall asleep when a smart assed representative from the insurance company told me I could stop twitching and moving my head and neck. It took everything I had to keep from unleashing on him. It would have never been physical, just verbal, but he was recording everything. All I wanted was proper treatment; they brought all this crap on… I never requested more than the attorney fees and treatment. So to the end of this situation I agreed to a settlement that was short of the medical bills because I was told they would appeal it for years to come. And to top all that off, I was still hurting!

I'm going to explain this so you will know the way I felt; being the coordinator for Crime Stoppers in Nacogdoches was more than a lot of work, it was a lot of public exposure as well. I was on television nightly and was on the radio constantly so my face and voice were familiar to the public in Nacogdoches as well as Lufkin because we shared a T V station. The coordinator in Lufkin was the same way. People read the stories in the paper and my name was in there over and over again. I made public appearances at events throughout the county and spoke to nearly every service or social club and organization that existed in Nacogdoches County. I knew a lot of people and a lot of people knew me. At that time I was the face of the Police Department and everywhere I went, people would speak and shake hands... and a lot of the time from people I had no idea who they were. But in that situation you just smile and say "Good to see you" or "How are you today?" It was like being a celebrity only in a small way and I liked it. But with that good side there is always a bad side.

People recognized you in Wal-Mart and would stop you and ask about a wreck that happened on the loop that day... I didn't even know there was a wreck. All you could do was tell them you weren't for sure, but the traffic officer would know the facts. I was questioned about why the police had a car pulled over... hell I didn't know. I was even asked if I could get a ticket taken care of... by someone I didn't know. I always tried to address these people with professional and yet friendly responses and I hope even today I was able to do that. I would be in a restaurant with my wife and some friends or the kids and people would point and some would walk over to the table to speak with me, but always about Police business. I wish more would have just asked how I was.

I have always enjoyed a cold Corona beer and lime with Mexican food, but now if I had one in the public then someone complained that I was out drinking heavily or drunk in public. I went to Lufkin one night to have dinner and some guy walked to the table where my wife and our friends were and looked at me then said "So it's okay for the police to drink, but not the plain folks, is that right" I didn't want to cause a scene so I replied "No sir, it's okay for plain folks to have a beer, too." It was good reports and then bad and somehow they always made it back to the department. I didn't drink heavy at all and never would I be found intoxicated out in the public. (Unlike Jamaica) My Chiefs both old and new were aware of my behavior in public and they dismissed the calls as bullshit. I cannot imagine what one's life would be like if they were really famous. Here I was a small town public figure and I hated the after-hours attention... well, not the positive attention because it was sort of cool. My department backed me, My Crime Stoppers board backed me and overall the public backed me. By this time though my wife didn't, she was tired, too.

So I requested to bow out of the Sergeant interview and just stay with Crime Stoppers. A new Sergeant was selected and I was called to the Chiefs office... he wanted to know why I pulled out. I explained to him my thoughts and feelings and he looked at me like I was crazy. He told me he didn't give that order and he had no intention of taking Crime Stoppers away from me, Sergeant or not. I was furious, I had been lied to and it was intentional. I told the Chief it was all okay I was happy being where I was. I kept on doing what I was doing. A new order came down in C.I.D. that no detective would get a reduced case load, I'm sure it was meant for me and I know it didn't come from the Chief.

One day while I was at the District Attorney's office filing a case, the DA told me he was in need of an investigator and wanted to know if I was interested. At first I thought no but then I wanted to know more about it. The pay would be actually a little more than I was making but... no weekends unless absolutely necessary, a take home vehicle and several other benefits that I liked. I got the information and did some heavy thinking. I tried to talk it over with my wife, but at that time she was too far gone from the marriage and even though she answered, she didn't care anymore. I was just too stupid to see it then. The following week I requested a meeting with the Chief and I was going to discuss my workload. If I was going to continue all the public relation type work I needed to have my case load reduced a little at least down to a ten hour type day.

I walked in his office and before I could say anything he said, "Glad you're here, I've been wanting to talk to you about taking on a role as one of the coordinators of the Explorer Post" Well shit... more work. I explained to him that I was looking for time to do what I had now and could he see if that was possible. He told me that as of then he didn't have a full time Public relations position available. He didn't have another detective slot available and had no idea of how long it would take to get those. He told me I would just have to tough it out. He wasn't ugly or mean about it at all in fact he was concerned. Like I mentioned, I was just out of gas and fading fast. I excused myself and called the DA to make sure the position was there and waiting and he replied it was and I could start after January first... it was December 15th then.

I re-entered the Chiefs office and told him I respected his position and understood he had to work within a budget but I just couldn't keep up the pace anymore. I gave my two week notice. That Chief told me he did not want me to leave and what could he do to make it right... I had already told the DA I would take the position. They did give me a very nice going away party and presented me with a service plaque. I had finally figured it out, I wasn't married to my wife, I was married to the Police Department and had to make a choice... but again it was too late already. So on December the 31st of 1999 I was no longer a Nacogdoches Police Officer. However on January 3, 2000, I was an Investigator with the 145th District Attorney's Office. Still the PO-PO!

Chapter 17

A whole new way to be a Police Officer was upon me and I was going to make the best of it. I showed up my first and had no clue what was expected of me. I would not be arresting people anymore, I would not be working cases assigned to me... I would be helping the prosecuting attorney's prepare for trial. I still had to leave Crime Stoppers and that was very hard for me to do. I had let the board know back in December but I still had a few episodes ready to film. I gave the information to the C.I.D. Lieutenant and helped him start preparing to do them before they found a replacement. I took the last commercial and when I signed off instead of saying "With the Nacogdoches Police Department, I'm Detective Kenny Hensley" I said "With the 145th District Attorney's Office I'm Investigator Kenny Hensley".

I thanked all the citizens of the county for the support they gave and the program and told them I was honored to represent them and I meant every word of it. The Crime Stoppers board gave me a nice farewell party and the DA allowed me to go to a final convention later on and once that was over, I was finished with Crime Stoppers. What I didn't know was before I would leave to the convention my wife and I after twenty three years of marriage would separate. What? If you could do twenty three, seems you could finish up but not to be, she was sick of living the life I gave her. After several attempts and the required time limit, our divorce was final and she didn't even have to be there.

Off to Corpus Christi for my final Crime Stoppers Conference and what a great time it was. We met up with the Lufkin people and really had a great time. I got to be really good friends with some of those that I was just an acquaintance with. I cannot thank them all enough... I even learned how to two-step, something I had never even wanted to learn before. I really hated to see the week end because of the treatment I was receiving and to top it off out program won more awards, icing on the cake. But all good things must end and the conference ended and we headed back to Nacogdoches. Back home nothing had changed and even though I fought it for a while, I was not going to save my marriage. My youngest son was now a senior in High School so after a long hard battle with myself, I accepted the facts and started to prepare myself to move on.

Back on the job it was time to get to work and like I said it was different. I was given a list of requests the prosecutor needed for a trial or even a plea bargain. Things like criminal histories and Pen packs (records of prisoners in TDC) I had to locate witnesses and get them to the office for interviews sometimes even by phone. I arraigned for travel and rental vehicles and hotel rooms. Other responsibilities were to drive to Houston as most of the people we flew in through Houston. I went to Houston so many times that the Police Department at the airport allowed me to park in their lot to keep from walking so far. I also was responsible for setting up for Grand Jury meetings. And get this... on the mornings of Grand Jury I had to go by Shipley's Doughnuts and bring them to the assembly... what a concept, a cop buying doughnuts! I was responsible for anything the prosecutor needed. There was nothing hard about it, nothing physically demanding... well except lifting them dough-nuts without grabbing one until after Grand Jury. I was out of the office quite a bit so no boredom and in ten years I had to work one Saturday, that's it.

Now the prosecutors were something else... not one made the same and as different as night and day. First of all they were intelligent, every one of them only in their own separate ways. The original DA that hired me was a great guy and loved to show his bling. From a famous family and worked with the Houston Police Department, he was outgoing and loved to buy things. I liked him and respected him, but I never was able to help him in trial because he didn't have one while he and I were there. The next one was a workaholic like me. He was so intelligent it was scary... memory of an elephant. When he set his mind to something he wouldn't back up until he finished. A local Doctor's son and ex- marine... working for him was a pleasure. Although he was way younger than me, I respected him to no end. Today he is a district judge and a damn good one.

The DA that followed was as nice a person as you would want to meet... just don't cross her. I loved working for her and thought very highly of her. She won some big cases that I had the honor of helping on. I would take her to interview people and we would wind up in some real crappy areas. The one thing above all others I will say about her is she truly cared about the victims and the way they were treated. I still keep in touch with her today and run across her every now and then... I miss not working with her. The assistant DA's were all different as well. Over ten years they ranged from super snob that knew everything to bat shit crazy Wildman. I really enjoyed working for most of them, however, there were some that I did not like at all. Some tried lots of cases and others didn't even do one trial the whole time I was there. One of them actually wrote a novel, I still have my autographed copy at home. And one of my favorites, passed away after suffering some sort of aneurism at work, I believe. I worked with two different investigators as different as night and day and a few secretaries and victim assistance people. There were times that we had a strong prosecuting team and I am proud that I was a part of that. I felt good when an attorney would ask for my opinion on something and several even read closing statements to me to get my feedback on them… I appreciated the fact they did that am glad I was able to help.

One of the biggest and most important trials in our county was a murder trial involving a spouse and her daughter with the help of a few local kids. Big news item and even got presented later on an episode of Snapped (television series). Our prosecutor was magnificent in trial… all four or three; oh hell it was a bunch. The same witnesses were needed for each trial so I had to re-subpoena them each time. She was relentless in trial and got convictions in every single one. Her closing arguments were tear tear-jerkers and they should have been. She not only succeeded in this trial there were several more major trials she would totally dominate like a home invasion case we worked. This involved several suspects entering a home to rob two men. They put pillow cases over their heads or maybe just wrapped them so they couldn't see. They threatened and pistol whipped these men. The defendants were so confident when they walked into the courtroom… in green and purple suits. By the time she was through with them they looked like whipped puppies. Guilty, guilty and guilty… boom, boom and boom. She also would be in charge of a murder trial that had our entire area interested, the one I refer to as the bridge murder.

This one was long, drawn out and the DA and I had to travel many miles to get everyone interviewed. A murder under a bridge right on the county line, just happen to have occurred on our side of the river. This case involved not only a victim, but his entire family. They were so helpful in our preparation for this trial. The DA was up against, in my opinion the number one defense attorneys in East Texas. This trial took months to prepare for and I was kept extremely busy however the prosecutor was even busier. The morning arrived for the trial to begin and we had assembled the witnesses, ready to go. The opening statements were presented and the two attorneys went to war. These two were friends outside the courtroom but inside was a different story. The prosecution was good and the defense was good. The trial went on and on as the witnesses testified one after the other. Then the closing statements and the jury went to deliberate.

I will say this about the DA and this defense attorney, they were both very good and I had witnessed them against each other several times. It was amazing at times to watch them in a courtroom. I have nothing but respect for both of them today and consider them friends. I hope the feelings are mutual. The verdict was back and we re-entered the courtroom… Guilty! Now for the punishment phase to begin. Again with the witnesses and testimony in order to access a fitting punishment. The DA would ask for something towards the top of the range and the defense would plead for something towards the bottom. To make a long story short… the jury decided on something towards the top. It was one of many great trials I had the honor of working on.

Although our office had a, shall I say, winning record? We did not win every trial. There was one that our office failed to win and part of the reason… lack of equipment. It was again a murder trial and all the witnesses had been brought in for the trial. The proceedings started and everything seemed like a normal trial. We had re-interviewed the witnesses and were assured by them that all the facts were on the table. There was a lady involved and a can of pepper spray. I won't go into the details of the case but there was also a video from the Sheriff's Office vehicle. We had watched time and time again on our monitors that were about 20 inches. And were confident of the testimony of the main witness but... this defense attorney had a huge television brought in to the courtroom, it was a very large screen maybe 60 inches or bigger. I told you I considered him the best defense attorney in East Texas... just an example of why. When the video was played on this huge screen it showed more area and it showed the witness had lied. The DA was furious with this lady and now she faced criminal charges as well. Like I mentioned before, this DA cared about the victims.

My marriage was over as the final papers were drawn and it was time for me to get a social life again. I had spare time with this position. With weekends off and mostly 8:00am to 5:00pm during the week, I had time to get out and do things. I did some really dumb things at first, like buy another Corvette. I don't understand why so many divorced men do this sort of thing but I did it none the less. My youngest son was out of school now and at college, my oldest was in college... hell I had a little time and a little money... so how about a new motorcycle? Sounded good to me and so it would be. Again, I don't know why I bought it; I was recovering from a car wreck at the time and really couldn't ride it anyway...duh! I took on more hours at Wal-Mart as an onsite officer. I had started this extra job when in C.I.D with the city. I had started seeing a few women and was enjoying the idea of what I was doing. One day I wanted to just get away for a week and so I invited a lady I was seeing to go to Cancun for Christmas… made it happen. A fun trip and it was a needed trip. After we returned it was back to normal and preparing for more trials.

I poured myself into my work while I was at work and lived pretty freely when I was not working. I sometimes got so involved with work; I went overboard with my actions. I felt that it was my job to insure the prosecutor had everything needed for a trial. Nothing should jump up out of nowhere and cause a surprise and I was proud of the fact that I was able to do that. However, there was a big turn-over in prosecutors for our county and not all of them liked that attitude. They all had different ideas of what they wanted so I had to do things sometimes just to redo them later. One particular assistant DA was very hard to get along with and would do things for herself then give me a request to do them. The problem was we did things differently. On the other hand another assistant DA was so easy to do things for and even though a thank you wasn't needed, it was given. This started out being the perfect job but with personnel changes came conflict and as always I blamed myself. After all I controlled what I did and how I responded to any situation.

I will go into one other great thing about the DA office… the conferences were fantastic. I attended one in Washing D.C. and was able to see my brother living in Virginia. All over the State of Texas; Houston, Dallas, San Antonio, Austin and even El Paso, there were conferences for Attorneys as well as Investigators. I attended gang conferences along with the normal ones and was really racking up my in service hours because I received credit for these gatherings. I sometimes took a guest along with me for the week. There were a lot of fun times at the conferences and I requested as many as I was allowed to attend. Now… I did attend the classes. It was a party, but there were classes offered and I attended them, every one of them. I always figured that the County had paid this bill for me and they expected me to be in these classes so I was. I had fun and it was a big party, but I took care of business when needed. My partner attended these conferences with me and he was a fun person to be around. A retired DPS narcotics officer that loved his whiskey… we had a lot of good times together.

Everything was going well, or I should say so-so but I thought many times that maybe I should have stayed at the city Police department. There were days I liked where I was and others not so much. I did have a lot of loyalty to the DA, but was very uneasy with one of the assistants. I placed trust in another one of the office workers but a stab in the back was on the horizon from that. I was questioning the county government, not the system but the people… too many lies and deceit from what I once considered honest folks. I believe I was losing a little faith in the powers that be. Maybe this experience is why I never tried to get involved in politics. My social life, however, was looking better. I had met a lady at Wal-Mart that I enjoyed being around and we started talking. She was going through a divorce and I respected that… we had some good conversations. We did begin seeing one another regularly and that would start up a whole new chapter in my life.

Chapter 18

Like I mentioned, everything was moving along at work and it seemed more and more cases than ever before kept coming in. I would be asked to prepare 10 or more trials for the same day and with two District Courts... well that's a lot of trials to get prepared. The list of witnesses sometimes was lengthy and contacting some of them was almost impossible. I had a request from a prosecutor to locate and subpoena a witness for a trial. I located the witness... in Iraq. He was in the military and on active duty. That prosecutor wanted him to be in Nacogdoches and didn't care where he was... tell that to the military during action on the ground, I promise they do not really care who wants them there. I had a witness that I had to fly from Atlanta, Georgia to Texas for a trial one time. I drove to Houston to get her (already had her room in Nacogdoches) and on the drive home was notified that a plea bargain had been agreed on. Wow... I had to get her on a return flight but not until the next day and so she stayed in the hotel in Nacogdoches. The following morning I had to drive her back to Houston to catch her flight. All that expense... sad, I realize sometimes it can't be helped but really?

I once arranged a flight from Colorado to Houston and brought the witness in for less than one minute of testimony, then had to take her back as well. I made that trip a lot and at all hours of the day and night. I am not complaining, I was getting paid to do it, just seemed wasteful sometimes. One more was a witness in North

Carolina that would not fly. Had to rent a car for them as her spouse joined her and let them drive… got a motel room and the trial was moved to another date. Back to North Carolina they went and we rescheduled… same old, same old and the second time was a repeat of the first. On the third call to this witness I was told that they were not coming and they didn't care what I did. She told me to put them in jail or whatever but they were not going through another trip.

One more before I move on… a witness for a trial was needed and I could not run him down. I finally located a family member and was told he was out of the country. At the persistence of the prosecutor, I requested a number to reach him and was told he is not reachable for a few more days… What? I left my number and asked if they would have him call. A few days later I got a call from the witness; he was in South America on some sort of expedition (I guess he was the real life Indiana Jones or something). I explained to him the situation and he just told me no way. In a last attempt to convince him I told him I had a subpoena for him and he sort of giggled and told me to come serve it. He was on a Sat Phone somewhere in a jungle. Don't misunderstand, most witnesses were easy to find and very cooperative but in ten years these few stood out.

The lady I had been seeing and I were getting serious, even though she was sixteen years younger than me. I in my mid- forties and she was thirty but we had a great relationship and one more little thing… she also had two young children. My oldest son, remember number One? Was about to graduate from SFA and the youngest child was four… oh, lord, had I lost my mind? The answer to that is NO. She had a five year old son and a four year old daughter… this little girl latched on to me like I had been around her whole life. The boy was a bit skeptical and kept his distance for a long time. In six months we would marry and start a new home. I had purchased a piece of property from some friends (more like family) and a new house was in the making.

One day, while she was making room in a closet, she came across one of my old raid uniforms. Solid black with the face hood and all... she started to wonder what she had married. I got home and she was asking all types of questions about that outfit. Once I explained we both laughed about it, but she still tells this story today.

My wife took an immediate fondness to my Mother and the rest of the family as well. As a matter of fact, my mother and she are so close these days you would think they had known each other their entire lives. She fit right in with everybody and so did those two little ones. I was feeling Family type again and I liked that feeling. Something was happening though... I had been working a lot as security for Wal-Mart and now was in the process of building a house... hell I was falling back in the same old routine. A brand new family and I was not home and off working all the time.

The pressures at work were getting worse and it was a lot my fault. I took everything so serious... after all we only handled felonies, right? I had the duty of working felony level hot checks as well and that was a lot of work. Anytime someone filed a hot check that exceeded $1200.00 dollars it was given to me to either file charges or work out a pay back. That amount was been raised since then but all criminal amount levels went up. Would you know the difference between a bad check and a hot check? Most people don't so it was my job to explain that. I got a positive response to my efforts as all but a very few didn't pay and were prosecuted. I worked cases from that $1200.00 mark up to $300,000.00 which was the largest I ever had. I always wondered how someone didn't know they were

$300,000.00 short in their account but then I never had that much in all my accounts combined and then doubled. Most always the writer would want to make it right and so a payback plan was set up… so it worked fairly well even though it was extra work load.

I wanted a little bit of a stress relief activity so I bought a new Harley Davidson Night Train. My wife and I were going to start riding with a group of people called the Blue Knights (Police Motorcycle club). We had all the gear and looked the part until one day, she and I decided to participate in a toy run. Toys for underprivileged kids, a great cause and was fun right up to the part when one of the ladies fell off the back of a bike after the one she was a passenger on hit another bike… she later died from those injuries. My wife lost all interest in riding then and it wasn't long until I sold the bike.

We finally were all moved in our new house and loved the country life. A fishing pond, hunting… we were very happy. The little boy I will call number three was coming out of his protective shell and number four (the baby girl) was as always, as sweet as she could be.

Life seemed to move along really nice and several years were gone before I knew it. I lost my college buddy to cancer and wrote a song for him. I was never a good guitar player but lyrics came easy and fortunately for me I had a lot of friends that were also great musicians. I would tell them how I wanted it to go and bang on my guitar for them and then like magic… they made come to life. My closest friend of the musicians was guitar buddy and he was a fabulous player .He played in a couple of bands mostly local along with piano buddy, bass buddy and a couple of drummer buddies. I knew several other guitar pickers who were so talented and all would help me. So we put together this song for his funeral… brought out many tears.

I wrote songs for my Dad, (see words to *Rocky* in back of book), my boys and my new daughter, even my wife and ex-wife, called it *Get On Your Broom And Ride*. Eventually, I would place all these songs on SoundCloud under Ken D. Hensley… still there. Song writing became a good stress reliever and I continued. I met a young girl from Diboll one day with a fantastic singing voice. I wrote a song called *Come Home to Me* about our soldiers in the Middle East and she put vocals to it with piano buddy providing the music. Well, you will just have to listen to it, I think it's that good. My stress level was dropping and when I stopped working my extra job at Wal-Mart it continued to go down. But somehow things just weren't right… I would find out soon why.

Everybody knows that feeling that something just isn't right and I had it at this time. The DA was up for re-election and the competition was an ex-assistant of hers. I respected and thought highly of both of them and didn't know what to say or who to say it to. I tried not to give any opinions to anyone about what I wanted to happen, talk about walking a fine line. I hated this situation and thought that if I just stayed out of it, I would be okay. I would not vote in the election and that way I could remain neutral. Boy was I wrong!

Each of these ladies had great up sides; they were both extremely smart and good at what they did. I had worked side by side with both of them in trial and can't say enough about their abilities. I witnessed the opposing candidate during a murder trial convince a jury that the victim was an angel when in fact he was just the opposite. She had a way of doing that and was really good at it. On the other hand, the current DA was a fantastic trial lawyer with a fantastic personality. She showed compassion for the victims like I told you earlier, they meant something to her. So, who do you chose? Remember I could not say no to certain things… well this particular time frame I will not go into deeply because of one thing I was taught growing up; If you can't say something good about someone, don't say anything at all.

After the election was over the opponent had won and when she reorganized her staff… I wasn't on it. So I ended my stop at the District Attorney's office after a ten year stay. To this day I still have the highest respect for my former boss. She is still a wonderful person and I will always be grateful she made me her Chief Investigator. The new DA, she is still a great prosecutor and I have respect for her abilities especially as a trial lawyer because I still feel she is one of the best.

There were two major national events that occurred while I was at the DA office. I was at home on February 1, 2003 and heard a loud sonic type boom. Shortly later I received a call from the Sheriff's Office that the Space Shuttle *Columbia* had exploded and they needed my help. I was sent to a location on state highway 21 and was to guard a sizable piece of the shuttle from be tampered with. I was at the first site in west Nacogdoches County and lots of people were trying to stop and take a look at the debris. I was at that post for eighteen hours straight, a heck of a long day but a necessary task. I was interviewed by several radio and television stations and had my picture in the Houston paper standing beside that piece of *Columbia*. I remember feeling very sad for the occupants of the shuttle and the impact that the incident had on America. It was a huge blow to our country and I won't forget the way I felt standing beside that piece of the shuttle.

I was at the office one morning on September 11, 2001 and the television was on in the conference room when I heard the breaking news that one of the towers at The World Trade Center had been struck by an aircraft. Then the other tower was hit and watched in horror and disbelief as the mighty twins crumbled to the ground. I was furious and angry... I was worried about the world situation and what my kids were to face. I called them both. I felt no different than most American citizens... there was no love lost there, I wanted revenge! All those first responder lives... all the citizen lives lost... all those AMERICAN lives lost. Yes, I wanted revenge and even though today I am calmer, I am one of the "Never Forget" crowd. God Bless America!

Have you ever listened to the song "He Went to Paris" by Jimmy Buffett? It sure makes a lot of sense now because time was flying by and I still had a lot to do. I was tired of my work and I know the reason why; I was a police officer and working in a DA office is not Police work. The job was part secretary, part baby sitter, part taxi driver, part travel agent, part caterer and so on and so on but very little police work. Maybe it was time for me to back off and relax a little. I could get on as reserve officer with a Constable and find something to do to make a living.

There were many differences between working for the City and working for the County. Both had their good and bad rules and regulations but one stood out that I never really understood. I was taught by my dad to always show up for work and never be late or miss if it can be avoided. I took pride in the fact that I was never late to work in my entire career... even through today. I always left my house early and arrived to my job ahead of nearly everyone. I would use that time to catch up on paperwork or read the news and of course, have a cup of coffee or six. I love my coffee in the mornings and afternoons. After a few years of doing this, it became a habit and was the normal daily routine. I also took pride in not missing work days as well. I showed up for work every day with the exception of maybe a few sick days and the days my kids were born.

Those sick days... hell, I thought I was dying. The city police department allowed an employee to accumulate sick days to a certain amount. I maxed out very quickly and tried to donate the days I was earning to go to people that needed them. The last few years I worked for the city I didn't earn a single day because I was at the limit. The beauty of this was when I resigned; I was able to draw a check for a portion of those days. I did in fact receive a very nice sized check for being at work. My loyalty and dedication paid off, even though, it was only a small percentage. I was reimbursed for unused sick days, vacation days and comp time as well so the city did exiting employees right or back then they did. I don't know what they do nowadays. I had a great experience with the city and appreciated the opportunity to work for them.

The county, on the other hand, didn't do so well. I practiced the same routine, never late, not missing any days and even staying late quite often all for nothing! I never received any comp time for the extra hours I worked either. When I departed from the county... I had to give it all back to them because they didn't pay for that type of compensation. Ten years of loyal, dependable service and it meant nothing. I was very disappointed in my county but, it is what it is and at that time it wasn't much at all. Understand that it wasn't employees of the county, there were many wonderful people working for the county and I was friends with most of them. It was a handful of the governing administrators that I lost faith in. But... we move on and forgive and forget, right?

I did have a take home vehicle for most for my twenty years with the city and county and I always considered that as part of my salary. The city car had way more restrictions than the county one did but overall it was a very important part of the jobs. I will say this... I witnessed several people that were furnished vehicles abuse that privilege, but I used my vehicle for work and work only. I did receive permission to drive my county vehicle to Wal-Mart while I worked off duty because it was on my way home and it didn't add any extra miles to the vehicle. I also took care of those vehicles. I had them serviced and kept them clean at all times. I laugh now because most of the vehicles I drove were old worn out patrol cars and with the county, a ten year old Ford Taurus... but they ran and got me where I needed to be including many trips out of town for seminars and training conferences. I was lucky to have been able to use these vehicles and do not recall a single time I abused that perk.

The city and county also had very different dress codes and this might not seem like much but it was to me. With the city, I was furnished a uniform to wear as well as most of the leather products and even a firearm if I chose to. In C.I.D. I was given $500.00 per year to purchase clothes to wear. We wore slacks and sport coats along with a tie. We could wear a suit if we chose, but most only did this on court days. I don't know if you have been shopping for clothes like that before but $500.00 doesn't buy much and the rest was up to the individual to pay for. It was, however, $500.00 dollars. I always carried my own weapon so there for I was responsible for the holster and a nice waist holster could cost $100.00. A shoulder holster in leather could run that high as well.

We were to keep our hair cut clean and only allowed to have a trimmed moustache. No beards at all! We were not allowed to wear blue jeans or colored jeans for that matter. I thought it was funny on the tie policy; a tie with a short sleeve shirt reminded me of Homer Simpson and never looked good to me at all. This policy was eased up a little when we were allowed to wear collared Polo shirts that were embroidered but that was as I was leaving so it didn't affect me.

The county, on the other hand, was again different. At least with the DA office it was. I was allowed to wear pretty much what I wanted as long as it was nice and I paid for it. I wore colored jeans, white shirts and boots most of the time. But I could wear slacks, pull overs with a collar, polo's and even blue jeans. The only rule was on court day, I was to be dressed professionally with a tie and coat and I always was. I was allowed to wear a beard or goatee as long as it was kept clean and trimmed and most of the time I was with the DA I wore the goatee. This proves that the county did some things better that the city, but remember, I was not in the public eye as much. Both had upsides and downsides and overall I guess my biggest complaint was my loss of faith with the county. Now days… I don't hold any grudges towards any one of them and believe they did what they thought was the right thing.

Chapter 19

I got a reserve position with a local Constable to keep my certification status intact. He had been a friend for many years and more than that was a great person, I was lucky he had a position available. I went out a couple of times a week with another deputy constable on patrol and started working as a police officer again. I was doing things that street officers do and loving it again. I found what I always wanted to be all over. I had gotten so wrapped up in climbing that success ladder that I had forgotten why I went into this profession. I was able to answer calls and back up other units, hell... I was back where I belonged. DWI one night, a fight another night and sometimes they happened in the same night. Assisting DPS with accidents... oh that brought back some memories but it made me feel alive again... made me feel needed again. I had one shortcoming... I needed a pay check (don't we all?). I checked around and there was really nothing available locally, so I thought I would do something until a position became available.

It's not easy looking for a new job when you are over fifty and I found that out the hard way. I was offered several positions but all were out of town and some were even out of the country. Remember I was raising a second family and had vowed to not let them grow up with me off somewhere working. Out of country was out of the question, but I will say that the pay did make me think about it... long hard hours and days of thinking about it. Shit, no way because my family was going to be priority number one. That included all my family, number one, number two, number three and baby girl, my wife and someone had to look after my mother... right? I had made that promise and I was going to keep it, period.

OK... let's get back in the saddle and make this work. I was going to keep working with the Constable's office and would find something to make a living at home. If it worked out, so be it and if not, so be it. I tried for weeks to find something I wanted or for that matter, something I could do for a pay check. I was very fortunate that my wife's adoptive (really just very close friends that we considered family) parents arranged an interview for me. I was going to try selling high end toys at an RV dealership. The economy was down but the people in the market for these travel trailers were mostly in the oil field business and it was booming.

Many retired people that wanted to do some traveling were also in the market so I thought... I can do this; I can make enough to keep things going and still get to work actively in law enforcement. I guess I was not recalling the time I tried being a salesman when the economy was down but it didn't take very long to remind me. The general manager of the dealership was a very nice person and he worked with me teaching me the techniques of selling these RV's. He tried to teach me how to sell them to people who didn't even want one. I tried to copy his style and persuasion with potential customers, but never really got it. He was good and so were his family members that worked there with him. His wife and two daughters also were there and in sales. I learned a lot from them but it wasn't the way I was raised to deal with people.

As hard as I tried to, I just could not bring myself to do the things that seemed necessary to sell these RV's at that time. Well it didn't take long before my ways and their ways crossed paths and so instead of causing a scene, I decided to just try my way and see where it took me. Again I was the first one at work every morning, hell I opened the store but because of the sales rotation... if a customer came in I could not sell them an RV unless it was my turn. It's funny how the people that give the most get the least... but that's the way it seems sometime. I also stayed and closed up every evening as well but that was the cop in me not wanting anyone there late due to the fact we closed after dark many nights.

I was going out at night with the Constable's office and having a blast being a police officer again and this started me to think about what was next on my list of things to try. I was happy again but with the hours required to selling the RV's, I was at work all the time. It seems if you missed a day, you missed a sale so working on Saturdays was on again and I had one week day and Sunday off. I was not getting that quality time with my family again because the kids were in school on my day off and so that left Sunday only for family time. I made some sales and had a couple of good pay checks that kept the bills paid for the time but I knew I wasn't cut out for this type of work. I needed to stay for a while longer until something else would come along for me.

There were several reasons I didn't fit in as a salesman and I had a hard time fitting in with the lifestyle. I liked being honest with people and I mean I don't like embellishing things to make them desirable. I am not saying or implying that the methods used were dishonest or that lies were told to make sales, I am just saying this; I worked hard for my money and I felt everyone else did as well so trying to get someone to give that money for something that is not what it was made out to be was wrong for me. Needless to say one day the manager's wife and I got cross with each other over something I refused to tell a customer. The manager, as nice as he was, pulled me aside and told me I had to comply with what she said. I began looking for a new position at that moment.

Again, there were offers that were located out of town and still some out of country that were available so I had to be patient and wait for something to open up. Of course, all of these were back in law enforcement and I wanted more and more to get back to what I did. The Constable's office was great but I wanted a full time position and there was just nothing open in Nacogdoches County at that time. I was told that as soon as there was an opening that I would have a job by several agencies but you know, sometimes a person has to be moving forward and not waiting. The more nights I went out, the more I wanted back in… I was a peace officer and that's what I needed to do. I had spent twenty years of my life in law enforcement and I had to get back to it. Twenty years? Really? I had been doing this for that long.

I went to see the chief of the school police department and applied for a position that was soon to be available. It took a long time for that to work out, but finally one day he called me. "Are you still interested in this job here?" he asked. It took me about one second after he spoke to answer… "Yes I am, when do I start?" He told me a date and so now I had two weeks to get everything ready to go back to where I belonged. I had some deals working at the RV store so I continued to go in every day but I did inform the manager I was leaving.

There was a situation with the RV store that really got my blood boiling though and it was a cocky know it all sales rep that dropped by every now and then to… show us how to move these rigs. He made the statement that he could sell anything to anybody even if they had no intentions of buying it. He was going to demonstrate his skills to us and the first customer he tried… well they didn't buy the RV. He acted like an ass and total jerk every time I saw him, but I understand he went to work for the owner later and pretty much is running the company or maybe he owns it. I don't really know and don't really care. I do know that he couldn't sell me water if I was dying of thirst and had a pocket full of money. Anyway, I was finished with him so I left the RV dealership, but not on the greatest terms. I really do not dislike anyone that worked there and as a matter of fact think highly of some of them… others just don't agree with my life rules and that's okay. They do what they have to do and I do what I have to do. I have to go home and sleep at night and so far I was able to do just that.

Chapter 20

The day finally rolled around that I was to report for work at the N.I.S.D. Police Department and I was more than ready. First things first… get any paperwork completed, get re-qualified with my weapons and then make a trip to Tyler, Texas for uniforms. After all that was completed, I was assigned a campus… Mike Moses Middle School. This was a 6th through 8th grade campus and was one of two middle schools in the district. Even though I had never been an officer on a school campus, I had been reading and asking questions about just how to be this type of officer, because it is different… very different. When I ordered my uniforms I was shocked at the sizes… what the hell? I had gone from a 32 inch waist to a 38 inch waist while at the DA's office… damn! I did manage to quit smoking after so many years of that disgusting habit. You know that it is said there is nothing worse than a reformed smoker… it might be true, it is true! Anyway while waiting on my uniforms to arrive I was shown all the different campuses and introduced to all the administrators at each one. I knew many of them from over the years and remember, I had sent two of my kids through this district. Speaking of that, it reminds me of the school years of my two oldest… they had it pretty rough sometimes when it came to dealing with the police. Most of the officers in town knew them and when they were found somewhere they weren't supposed to be… they had a choice to make. "You call him and tell him or I will, which will it be?"

This happened on more than one occasion, hell more than several occasions... I am laughing thinking about this now! My oldest two boys were no different than any other teenagers of that era. They made the same mistakes and were involved in just as much as the rest of their classmates. I have been told by them that while they were growing up, they were teased about who their father was... the po-lice, Po-Po and any other word used to describe the officers. They tell me that they got caught many times with alcohol and were stopped quite a few times as well.

Once in a bar, my youngest was approached by an officer and he said..."Mr. Hensley, think your daddy knows where you are tonight?" He could only respond..."No, but I think he's about to." I think back and remember the teenagers I gave a break to years ago and they seemed to be doing well. They also had a few bad days at school and fortunately those were taken care of by the school.

One of my boys has a scrapbook and I was flipping through it one day recently... found a detention slip from the assistant principal at the campus I was assigned to. We had known each other for years, as he was also my youngest boy's (well number two anyway) coach as he was growing up. One day, while still with the DA, I was given a video to watch and see if I was able to identify any of the high school students involved in the feature film. This film was of high school students at parties and drinking as well as numerous fights that were videoed. As soon as it started I recognized the voice of the cameraman… you guessed it, my son (number two). Are you serious? My son of all people was the narrator of this documentary. Then on top of that, I also knew most of the stars of this Hollywood production because they were friends of my sons and so… when the officer needing the information came back to pick up the video…

I told him who they were and who the parents were including me! Anyway I must say that growing up as a police officer's child can be a little hard on a kid because not only do people expect perfection from officers, they expect it from their families as well.

That's another subject that needs to be explained… perfection. Why are police officers held to a standard that no one else is? I realize we carry guns but in today's world, who doesn't? I realize we may have to make life and death decisions and sometimes in split seconds, while the courts have months and years to figure a situation out and determine what should have been done. Not all people, but many wonder why we don't make a correct medical call… hell we're not doctors. Why would a doctor work for police wages?

Truth is… we are not perfect by any means, we are just people and we do make mistakes. I have found over the years that my opinion means nothing… why do all the other opinions mean something then? I am not allowed to get angry or upset and heaven help me if I offend someone, about anything… anything! I am expected to stand tall and take a cursing and all the while show no signs of emotion. I have been told that this is the way all professionals are treated and I disagree. Maybe I am wrong, but from my experience I don't feel this way. I have been degraded and even down right insulted during criminal trials. I was once accused of forging a signature on a confession… really? Like I would risk my career on a chicken shit burglary case or any other case as far as that goes. I tried every single day I went to work to do the very best I could for my profession and I wouldn't lie for anyone but I am far from perfect. As a matter of fact, I don't think anyone is perfect. I have been able to live with that for nearly sixty years so far and will continue until I take my last breath. Okay… no more preaching and on with the story.

I only had to respond to the school my son (number three) and baby girl went to twice, one trip for each child. The first time was when my son caused some disruptions at school. He came home and told me what had happened and I thought to myself… why would he be in trouble? But having already raised two boys, I knew there could be a hidden story in there somewhere. I contacted the principal and set up a meeting. Being the cop that I was though, I did a little investigating into the problem and after speaking with others involved I had some questions that needed to be answered before making a decision.

I gave the principal his time and he explained what he had been told. I told him that my son was capable of doing what he was accused of, but he normally didn't lie to me. I asked if he had looked into the situation and he told me only what the teacher had told him. That principal got the drift of where I was going with the meeting and together we decided to bring this to an end. After all we both wanted the same thing… we both wanted the right thing to be done. Together we had the teacher and my son report to the office and there they were, face to face. That principal requested that the teacher tell him again what had happened and… a totally different story came out. So the problem was resolved and when asked if I wanted my son removed from the class, I said no, they have to learn. I admired that principal for handling that the way he did. The only other time I had to go there was because of a foul mouthed coach who would rather climb a thorn tree and tell a lie than stand on the ground and tell the truth. Unfortunately, this situation has not been resolved… my opinion, too many relatives involved.

Back at the middle school… I was starting to place things in order and was ready to set up my office. The chief handed me a wad of keys about the size of a soccer ball and told me what a couple went to and figure out the rest... funny, right? Took around a month to get them all placed where they belonged, but I got it. Now to set up an office and as normal it was a makeshift conglomerate of furniture that matched nothing and certainly not each other. It took a few weeks but between the custodians, assistant principal and I, we put together a presentable office. Now... what does a school police officer do? I don't know, never been one, but it had to be similar to a regular police officer... answer is nope! This would be a totally different approach to law enforcement and I had a lot to learn, not about the law but procedure with these juveniles. Just when I thought I had everything figured out... I didn't know shit but was willing to learn. I soaked up information from the other experienced officers with the school district to the point that they probably hated to see my number on their phones. I truly wanted to do this right and the way the school district expected. I was back into my beloved law enforcement and I was in 100%.

The other officers helped so much... and one officer in particular helped me adapt to the way of a school police, she worked with me endlessly and I admired her for that. I knew how to investigate a theft, a burglary, an assault and even a murder and could prepare all for trial but the knowledge they had was important right now. I was able to work with them on certain different calls and eventually started to pick up the techniques used for campus policing. I had to polish up my juvenile law procedures along with the ways to deal with a preschooler to a high school senior and everything in between.

And... then there were the angry parent situations that would pop up every now and then, some of which would be challenging.

When I first came in, I was sent to several elementary schools to deal with unruly students... what a trip some of those were, I mean they could get crazy. For example; a young boy at an elementary school had some issues with his medication and when this occurred he just went ballistic. He would throw furniture around and destroy offices and... sometimes even strike those trying to help him. I had to sit on the floor and hold that student, calming him down until his parent arrived to take control of him. That young man broke a pair of $400.00 glasses that I had to replace. He didn't do it on purpose but they still were broke. There were several students that displayed this type of behavior and controlling them without harming them was a stressful and sometimes difficult task but I seemed to be able to do just that.

Another incident occurred at the middle school about the second week I was there. A student maybe twelve years old was mad at the assistant principal and swung his back pack at him, however, he did not make contact. I was in the hallway and as that student exited the office, he swung his fist at me. He missed but I was able to deflect his fist and spun him to the ground. Once he calmed down and we had his parent there he was fine. To this day that young man still goes out of his way to speak to me. He stayed in trouble most of his time in school with us but never with me. I wasn't ugly or overpowering to him, I just let him know that his behavior would not be tolerated.

Dealing with kids and young adults is a balancing act to say the least. I am from a family full of teachers and educators and had listened to stories of school incidents my whole life, but I had no idea that they were true! I have a great respect for our educators these days as they face situations and problems that are quite different than a few years ago. When I talk about the student body please remember that it is not one hundred percent of the students that are difficult to deal with, it is actually a small percent... a very small percent. It seems that the good always outweighs the bad, but the bad stands out among the good. Read a newspaper and count the stories... you will find that negative type stories are far more common than feel good stories. Watch the news... same thing. Who committed what crime and who caused problems and not so much on who accomplished a good deed. When we hear of or read a feel good story though, it is a relief and at least I renew my faith in mankind. The school system is no different but before I go on I want to say that in my opinion my school district does everything possible to make things better for the students, I mean they really go above and beyond to accommodate these kids.

School policing requires many talents and skills that are practiced every day and by that I mean; I have been in front of many classes talking about bullying, drugs, truancy and several other topics to the students. I worked with administration on the campuses and helped train on how to cope or deal with outside threats that now are a part of our schools. The dangers on today's campuses are real and can happen anywhere or anytime... to any school. One of our duties is to prepare the campuses the best we can for such an incident and pray it never happens. (Yes, I used the word pray) These students today are taught not only fire drills like years ago, but also evacuation drills. How to get out of a building and... how to be safe if trapped in a building are taught too. Every year there seems to be a new type threat to our students and school administration working with the school police address these problems... I am proud to be a part of that.

Outside agencies get involved by reinforcing the school agency and other things like providing drug dogs for inspections. They are under policy restrictions but play a very important role in controlling the drug problem in school. Before I go any further... there are some drug problems in schools and I believe you will find out that is nationwide. Again, that small percentage of problem students gets the attention.

One of the most practiced events that school police with every other agency are drilled on is the "Active shooter on campus." My gosh, this is the worst nightmare of anyone involved with a school at any level. I bring this up because sometimes as I talk with people about this subject... they are in disbelief that anything like this could occur at their school. I feel pretty certain that is the way people felt at one of many school shootings that have tragically occurred in this country. I was chosen to arrange this type of training as well as firearms qualifications for our department. I was fortunate to have friended a true professional in this field and with his additional instructors, our school buildings are used yearly for shooter and hostage rescue training. One of my duties is to keep our school officers qualified with their firearms and I take that duty very seriously. I have our officers go to the firing range at least twice a year and three times if I can to practice fine tuning their shooting skills. We shoot in the cold of winter and the heat of summer... bad people don't care about the weather. My hopes are in the event of such a catastrophic act, our department will be as ready as possible to deal with it in a safe and professional manner. As they say... when all else fails... trust your training!

At the middle school level, I dealt with mostly fights, fights and more fights. At one time the state allowed for school officers to issue citations to students for several different offenses. They could be cited for fighting, disrupting a classroom, offensive language and several other class C type offenses. This system seemed to work at our schools as we didn't have many second time offenders... a few but not many. If two students fought in school they would be cited for Disorderly Conduct. Of course there were exceptions and each confrontation was investigated before charges were filed. If a student did something in a classroom that caused the teacher to stop instruction of the other students... Disrupting a Classroom could be filed. We had kids throw desk and chairs across the rooms and this is what was filed unless it struck another student or teacher. When a student cursed a teacher or administrator... we filed Offensive language charges. Again, remember that only a very small percentage of the student body committed these offenses but when they occurred, we handled them as well as the school discipline that came with our charges. Students and their parents were cited in to court for truancy charges because it was a criminal act at the time.

Our local judges attempted several methods to try teach these students better choices... they would have them perform some sort of community service for a nonprofit organization or pick up cans and turn them in for money to donate to an organization. My favorite judge told them this and I quote,"I want you to pick up aluminum cans from the area and when you collect five hundred of them... take them to a recycle center and turn them in for cash. Then I want you to give that cash away to a nonprofit organization." When the student would look at her funny, she would tell them,"You don't have a job but your parent has to work hard for you, buying clothes and food and any luxuries you have so when you get fined then your parent feels like they are throwing away that hard earned money. So you need to know how they feel... work hard and then just give it away." She also outright fined some; it all depended on the elements of the case.

I realize that the State of Texas has since changed these laws but I am telling you… they worked! Now, the schools are responsible for handling most of the offenses, but there are a few exceptions. I may not be able to cite a student under 16 for a class C crime, but if that student is at least 13 and in the seventh grade or above, I am able to file papers at the court to have them served and appear before the judge. Did you get all that? It now takes an hour or so and a pile of paperwork to file a class C on a student in that age range. This has plus and minus affects but I am not a politician so I won't go into that subject any deeper.

The middle school level was full of surprises too… some of the stories I heard were hilarious and yet some were very sad. Never knowing what would come out of the mouth of a middle school student made the days interesting and sometimes I would just shake my head. All and all though, I couldn't help but really like most of these kids and many times what they told me reminded me of… Me! I remember telling several of them a saying my dad said to me…"That didn't work for me either back over forty years ago." I did have days that I wished I had stayed home… I hated arresting a kid, still do.

I did and do have to make arrests on occasion and most of the time would have to transport theses students to a juvenile detention center if the situation called for it. The detention center our county used was a little over an hour away and all the way to the facility the student and I usually talked. Most of these kids were smart and alert and, well they made a mistake. Trying to grow up too fast and "Be Cool" and whatever is said in today's society seemed to be the downfall for most of them. I hated why we were talking but enjoyed getting to know so many of those kids were enlightening experiences. Nearly every one of them that were first time offenders did not have a clue of what the detention center was like and that was one of the first things I got asked every time. I did my best to explain to them what was about to happen to them and when they realized that they were headed for basically, a jail for kids. This is the point when most of them started really paying attention and the questions begin to pile up. It was one of the worst feelings to me to drive away from that detention center and leave that student behind. I hated it but it was something I have to do even today. I can't remember how many times I had to make that trip but it was quite a few over the years.

Of all the trips I have made to the detention center, two stand out from all the others but not because of the crime committed; it was the talk with the student on the trip and events that occurred. The first one was a female student that was charged with an assault of a public servant (she struck a teacher) and really she wasn't a bad student; she just didn't think of what was happening... She still committed the assault though. We talked all the way and she was pleasant to talk with and seemed to have a level head on her shoulders to the point that I wondered how she actually did what she did. Now maybe she was a good actress, but she seemed very sincere as I explained the procedures to her. I told her when we arrived that I would escort her through a security door and into a secure waiting area. She would then be taken by me through the next security door where she would be searched and have a detection wand moved around her, this was to be done for the protection of employees and the juveniles as well. The attendant would remove my handcuffs and she would be processed in as I filled out some required paperwork. Then I told her I would leave for Nacogdoches and she would be transported by the Sheriff's Office from now on. She looked at me and seemed scared and even though she had earned this trip herself, the look on her face just tore me up. Then as I was leaving and told her to be good for me and I would see her back in Nacogdoches… the eyes got me again because she realized I was actually leaving her there. I know this may seem silly, but I hated leaving her there.

The second was a young man that had an illegal substance in his pants. He and I didn't talk so much, but when we did he talked about his family and what his mother must think of him. He told me that she didn't know what he did and he was not proud that his behavior and actions were going to hurt her. I was agreeing with him and said that my own mother would be hurt as well. Maybe they could use this as a new starting point, trying to get him to think more of himself so he would have a positive outlook. I told him he may not be able to change the past, but he could mold the future. Again, he may have been a great actor, but he appeared sincere as well. Now the problem began when we were inside the center… one of the juvenile posted up on an employee. It wasn't a pretty sight, but I think it hit hard with my juvenile. I do know that he has not been in trouble since that incident and I have told him several times that I was very proud of his transformation… I just hope it's for real!

Chapter 21

My home and social life were taking a turn for the better... I was able to spend time at home with number three and baby girl. I was able to attend so many of their school functions and enjoyed my spare time working around our place and fishing in the ponds. Number three wasn't into school activities as heavy as Baby girl, but he liked welding and shop and his AG classes. Baby girl was into everything she could possibly get in to. She plays basketball, softball and was a cheerleader on top of all that. She participated in track events and then she also made great grades (National Honor Society.) Just going to her events kept my wife and I busy nearly every afternoon and still does.

My two boys, number one and number two both had gotten married and were working at the business my ex-wife and her husband now owned. They were buying houses and getting started in their lives as adults and I was so proud of all my kids at this point... I only wished I would have designated more time to the first two. During this period, I also became a grandpa... yep my oldest, number one and my wonderful daughter-n-law had the first grandchild... wow... never in my dreams could I imagine this wonderful feeling. It's funny because we were all at the hospital waiting and waiting for the birth and Baby girl had to be in a town about thirty miles away to cheer at a football game. We continued to wait and at the last possible minute, we had to leave to get her there on time. We were no more than ten minutes from Nacogdoches when we got the call that our grandson had made his debut. We had to wait until after the game to get to see that little miracle. He was worth the wait.

Number three was now a senior in high school and damn… I was getting old! Baby girl was still involved in everything until she decided to take some college courses. Then she dropped her cheering position as co- captain of the squad to devote her concentration on education. She had decided she wanted to be Nurse Practitioner and set herself a list of goals to achieve. We were still busy during basketball and softball seasons. Now… we were getting to keep Grandson One for weekends and I was able to finally devote the time needed for a family. So what happened next? You guessed it… a second grandchild is on the way. Number one and Daughter-n-law were going to have another… BOY! Grandson Two would come into our lives and double our delight. I was learning now what my dad had told me long ago… family was everything, period! So to sum it up I am so very proud and love all my kids… first batch, second batch, married in batch and finally, the grand babies. I guess the only low points were all my mother's surgeries she had to endure and the loss of my own Grandpa… ninety seven years young.

Everything seemed to be going along fine at this time and the middle school problems kept on… mostly the same thing day in and day out. The fights continued but at that age it's not unusual except for one thing… it was mostly girls doing the fighting. When I was in school, all the way to high school, very few girls got into fights at school. As a matter of fact, I only remember one in junior high and none in high school. When a couple of boys would get in a fight the coaches were called in and the boys were taken to the gym. They placed boxing gloves on them and let them fight, supervised of course. The winner would receive one pop and the loser... three. That would be considered barbaric these days and totally unacceptable, I'm sure a lawsuit would get filed. Well let's face the truth, kids fight and you know what? So do adults! Kids bring habits from home and kids act just like their parents do at times. Example:

While a detective with the city I had to make contact with a victim of a physical crime. I stepped upon the front porch and a small child was standing behind a screen door looking at me. I looked down and asked him if his mom was home. This child was talking to someone and I heard from another part of the house "Who is it?" That little kid who couldn't have been three years old yelled back. "It's the "effin" police." Now I am far from being the perfect parent, but is this what an adult would want to teach a child?

I have heard the story way too many times of how a student was defending themselves because their parent told them if someone hit them... that meant they could beat the crap out of that person and that was self-defense, Right? Look up self-defense and you will find a totally different meaning is attached to the word. I have had the conversation with parents as to why their child was being filed on or a citation written. I have been told on more than one occasion that the student had the right to fight back and I agree right up to the point that the victim becomes the aggressor then we have a dual participant fight.

Sometimes a teacher will be injured attempting to break the violators up, now what? It just got raised to another level and additional charges. I handle each fight on its own merits and treat them all the same and I don't care who the fighters are or who their parents are. I will say this about the biggest majority of the parents though... they are cooperative and want the right thing done even if it causes them problems. Only a handful is unwilling to believe their children could not make a mistake or a bad choice. My view is all kids are capable of both acceptable and unacceptable behavior… it's a choice they make and they should be held responsible for the consequences, either way. . And parents need to stop telling young children, when they see an officer "You better behave or that policeman is going to take you to jail" It is the parents job to discipline their children not the police. It just makes kids afraid of officers for no reason. That officer would give his life to save a child, not hurt one. I hate it when parents tell their kids that.

As I write this I am still employed by N.I.S.D. Police Department and still loving my job. I am now on the high school campus and it brings its own challenges as well. I still have to make an arrest every now and then and deal with upset parents, but it is what I do. I will say it never gets boring and most days fly by. Like I said earlier, I am going to be sixty later this year but plan on working as long as I feel good about going in every morning or until the district runs me off… whichever comes first. I do tell you that while I'm writing this my chief decided to retire. Many people wanted to know if I would try for the position… answer is no. I am happy again and I spend time with my family and well… not interested.

There is one thing that disturbs me about being at a school… nothing to do with the district or staff, however. I see so much waste through our cafeterias. So much food thrown in a trash can. I have witnessed time and time again a student get a full plate of food and walk straight to a trash can and throw it in. I don't think I will ever get used to that behavior. Hopefully, I have not offended anyone with these few words I have put together but if I did, I just did. I have a great family both at home and at work and… I know it. So now

I have only a few things left to write down; questions I have been asked throughout my career so far… and about my injuries.

Chapter 22

Number one question asked of police officers... can you guess it? If you thought "Have you ever had to shoot someone" then you would be correct. Even children want to know the answer to that question. I am not sure why but I would venture to say I have been asked that ten times more than all others combined. My answer for all these years so far is a question... Does it matter? Why does that matter to anyone but me? The truth is I would say I have been very fortunate in my career even though it's not over yet.

Other questions; Have you pointed your gun at someone? Yes I have and on more than one occasion. What's it like to work a murder or death of a person? It's hard and sometimes stressful. It's not easy on the eyes or other senses but you have to pull yourself together and bring closure for the victim and the family. They are all different and you must take each one separately because there is no stencil to use.

Have you ever been shot at? I don't know for sure if it was actually at me or just in the direction I was in but I do know what a bullet zipping by you sounds like. I can go on and on but you get the type of stuff I am asked daily by people who don't know.

Did you ever hurt someone? Not on purpose, well that's not true, I did sort of go off on the guy who beat those kids a long time ago.

And I always liked... have you ever arrested someone? Hundreds of times throughout my career and don't have any regrets.

One last one is, How does it feel to get to drive fast? I have only had one high speed chase in my years so far and it was when I was in training... scared the shit out of me. The only thing I liked to ride fast were my dirt bikes, when I was a teenager. Hell, my kids (all of them) call me "Old Grandpa" and "Slow Poke" because of the way I drive so I hope that satisfies that question.

I saved these for last because they are what inspired me to write this whole thing... What type of person becomes a police officer? And... What type of people make the best police officers?

These are my favorite two questions of all time and here is my opinion. A person that becomes a police officer is very simply a normal person that answers a call for the job. The same type of people that make plumbers and carpenters... and even bricklayers. The same type that make doctors, lawyers and business operators or owners. The same type that work at Wal-Mart, Kmart, McDonalds and a thousand other ways to make a living. Normal people who rise to the cause... pretty simple huh? This question is the reason for this article; this is me... a cop by choice and what type of person I am. Everyone has a story and every story is worth reading or listening to... at least to me.

The next question is even more simple, what type of people make the best police officer? People who believe in what they do. Can't be any easier than that and yes, I believe. And finally... "Would you do it again if given the opportunity?" A good ol' East Texas answer for this question... Not just yeah, but... Hell yeah! Oh, and I almost forgot... it certainly is not for the money because there is very little of that. That is why cops are seen working extra jobs everywhere, now you know.

I did suffer a few injuries over the years and none of them were life threatening in any manner. The vehicle accident that injured my neck... I'm glad that healed up. I have broken my hand and several fingers making an arrest. I have dislocated my thumb and index finger so many times I lost count as well as broken my wrist. Seems like a lot of hand injuries and I feel it today especially in cold weather. I got hit in the knee with a baton by another officer one time so hard I couldn't walk for a couple of days, turned all black and blue and green and purple... it was a rainbow! A few cuts and bruises and a scrape here and there but nothing a few stitches and an ice pack didn't fix. A hip injury that plagues me today I suffered during a very physical arrest a few years back. I broke two ribs when two fighting people fell on top of me at a movie theatre. One was around 250 pounds, the other around 200 and they fell on me causing the armrest of a seat to crush against my side. I could not breathe for several seconds but fortunately he was arrested... with a little help from some pepper spray.

That reminds me of something else you may not know... so allow me to share this; if you see an officer carrying pepper spray or a taser then you should know that officer had one used on them. In order to carry either as an officer you must attend a training course and be sprayed by the capsicum and shocked with a taser... really! For me, that spray was the worst thing ever... holy shit! I never want to do that again. It would just not stop burning.

Me... I spend my spare time with my kids even though they are mostly grown and with my grandchildren, the lights of my life. I teach people how to shoot... accurately! Friends and family on the firing range learning to protect themselves from what our world has become and is to be. I believe that many of our fears are for real and that people have the right to defend themselves from aggression. I hope to be able to take my wife on a really nice vacation one day though…a cruise maybe. We never had the opportunity to go on a honeymoon. Here's a thought; maybe I should start hunting for Bigfoot (but not to hurt him). My wife gets a laugh out of me saying that.

I still have a year to watch my daughter play her sports if she continues to play before she heads to college. I ask in prayer to be able to spend many more years with my mom next door and our adopted parents down the road. A mother, wife, sons, daughter, daughter-n-laws, and grandkids are my reasons to get up every morning. Life would be empty without them.

As I wind this down, I want to say, "Thank you, Nacogdoches, for allowing me to serve you." I am proud to be a part of this town and community and look forward to a few more years if that's in God's plan. I have made many friends throughout my stay here and each one of them holds a place in my heart. I have helped many people through some hard and difficult times.

I make no apologies except to my kids who I denied some precious time to, I can never give it back, my boys, but I can try to make tomorrow better. I make no excuses, I have arrested many people and I believe in my heart that each and every one of them deserved to be arrested. I helped place a few in prisons because that's where they belonged. I see people in a store and they remember an encounter with me… sometimes I don't know whether to shake a hand or pull a gun but so far, it's only been hand shaking.

I've even had a few thank me for starting them on the right track… wow! My biggest compliment came from a high school student that told me he wanted to be like… me, another WOW! He wants to be like me? I can't imagine a bigger compliment than that because that's the way I've felt my whole life towards my dad. I never did get that mansion in River Oaks, but it was never about money anyway. I did get something just as good and maybe even better… a home. I have had better than some and not as good as others. I tried not to fall in that category of cops that can't stay married, but hey, I'm one and one in that department and everybody involved is happier now for it. I have won battles and lost some as well.

I said before I made some good friends and unfortunately a few enemies along the way. I have laughed and I have cried, I have been scared and nervous but stepped up to the plate when I was called upon. I am what I am, a Police Officer. All and all, life has been good to me and I thank God for that… I respect and salute all first responders and my brothers and sisters that form that Thin Blue Line by choice. And one more time,

Thank you…

By Choice © 2016

Epilogue

Rocky

© 2002

My first steps, he held my hand

Whatever I did, he'd understand

Christmas mornings, his Santa eyes

Watched me play and act surprised

Then as I grew, he did too

Those troubled years he helped me through

His gentle hands were oh so strong

This man to me could do no wrong

He worked and gave, never complained

Do what's right…he'd explain

What I would give for what he had

Most called him Rocky but I…I called him Dad

He touched the lives of young and old

The stories he told were solid gold

And even though he now is gone

In my heart…he will live on

He worked and gave, never complained

Do what's right…he'd explain

What I would give for what he had

Most called him Rocky but I…I called him Dad

Most called him Rocky but I…I called him Dad

A very special thanks to Sharron Randall. Thank you JP Luna and family as well as all the friends that read and critiqued this for me.

Dedicated to the memory of my dad... K.H. "Rocky" Hensley

Written for my wife, kids, grandkids and of course, my mom. Love you all so much.